New England's
VIKING AND INDIAN WARS

When I was a state representative in the Great and General Court of Massachusetts, the *Wampanoag Indians* came before the Committee of Natural Resources, of which I was a member. Their *Sachem, Lorenzo Jeffers,* wearing full head-dress, argued for land at *Mashpee,* which the English settlers had taken from the *Wampanoags* in the 1600s. The Committee listened many hours to *Lorenzo,* then we dismissed the Indians from the committee-room, and sat in *"closed session."* During this session, many of the members told *"Indian jokes,"* then we took a vote on Indian land-rights. The *Wampanoags* lost the vote 9 to 2, myself and Greg Mayhew, the representative from Martha's Vineyard, the only two voting for the Indians.

At the end of this closed-meeting, the Indian jokes still flying around the room, I stood up and told the other members that I was insulted. *"My mother is a Micmac Indian,"* I said, *"and I will not stand to hear one more Indian joke!"* I then stomped out of the meeting, with the Chairman of the Committee close on my heels, spouting apologies. I waited until the next morning to tell my obviously embarrased Chairman that *"I am as Irish as Patty's pig, and just look Indian, but I stopped those damned Indian jokes, now didn't I?"* The chairman was furious.

When I visited Cape Cod the following summer, to the pride of my children, *Lorenzo,* at a *Mashpee Powow,* invited me to smoke the peacepipe with him — for that honor, I dedicate this book to the now deceased *Lorenzo Jeffers, Chief of the Wampanoags.*

Bob Cahill

D1561723

COVER:

A painting, "THROUGH THE FIRE", *by Ken Schmidt, photo by Steve Harwood, courtesy of Lone Feather Studio, Ballston Spa, New York*

ISBN-0-916787-11-7

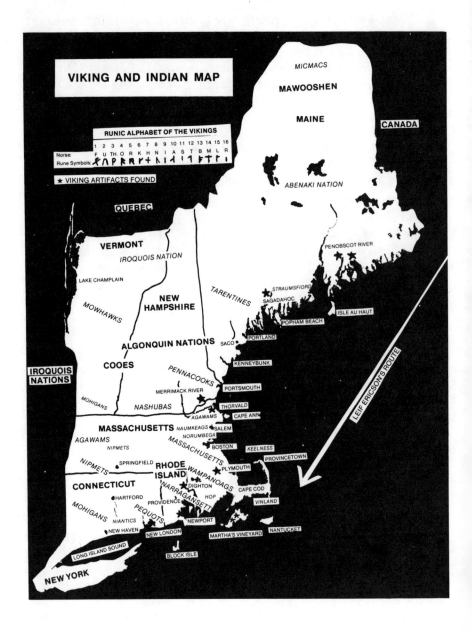

VIKING AND INDIAN MAP

MICMACS

MAWOOSHEN

MAINE

CANADA

RUNIC ALPHABET OF THE VIKINGS

	1	2	3	4	5	6	7	8	9	10	11	12	13	14	15	16
Norse:	F	U	TH	O	R	K	H	N	I	A	S	T	B	M	L	R

Rune Symbols:

★ VIKING ARTIFACTS FOUND

ABENAKI NATION

QUEBEC

VERMONT

IROQUOIS NATION

PENOBSCOT RIVER

LAKE CHAMPLAIN

NEW HAMPSHIRE

TARENTINES

STRAUMSFIORD
SAGADAHOC

ISLE AU HAUT

MOWHAWKS

POPHAM BEACH

ALGONQUIN NATIONS

SACO

PORTLAND

IROQUOIS NATIONS

COOES

KENNEYBUNK

PENNACOOKS

MERRIMACK RIVER

PORTSMOUTH

MOHIGANS

NASHUBAS

THORVALD

AGAWAMS

CAPE ANN

MASSACHUSETTS

NAUMKEAGS

SALEM

NORUMBEGA

AGAWAMS

MASSACHUSETTS

NIPMETS

BOSTON

KEELNESS

NIPMETS

SPRINGFIELD

PROVINCETOWN

RHODE ISLAND

WAMPANOAGS

PLYMOUTH

CONNECTICUT

NARRAGANSETT

DIGHTON

HOP

CAPE COD

MOHIGANS

HARTFORD

PROVIDENCE

VINLAND

NIANTICS

PEQUOTS

NEWPORT

NEW HAVEN

NEW LONDON

MARTHA'S VINEYARD

NANTUCKET

LONG ISLAND SOUND

BLOCK ISLE

NEW YORK

LEIF ERICSON'S ROUTE

I
VIKING VICTORIES OF VINLAND

"Protect us from the wrath of the Northmen, O Lord," was the constant prayer of the Irish, Scots, English, French, Italians, Spanish, Russians and Arabs, for some 200 years, beginning about 800 A.D. The Northmen, also known as Norsemen or Vikings, came swooping down from Scandanavia in their one-masted longboats, attacking coastal villages, confiscating food, material goods and women. These bands of blood-thirsty pirates from the *"creeks"* of Norway, Denmark and Sweden, conquered Western Russia, occupied half of England, over-ran Normandy in France, fortified the coastal cities of Ireland, and plundered Arab seaports in the Mediterranean. Wielding spears, broad swords, and great battle-axes that could lob off a head with one swing, they were considered the fiercest and most ruthless warriors of their time. They were also the best seamen and shipbuilders in the world.

At many of the coastal and riverside communities they controlled in Normandy, England, and Ireland especially, they settled in and built trading communities. In about the year 870 A.D., some Norwegian Vikings decided to settle into a large volcanic island they discovered in the North Atlantic, located 600 miles North of Ireland — known today as Iceland. When they arrived with their baggage from Norway, they discovered that other people lived there. They were called *"Scotties"* and had moved into Iceland over 100 years before the Norsemen. Most of the *"Scotties"* were Irish monks, who had left Ireland when the Vikings had attacked and destroyed their coastal monasteries. These Irish *"Culdees,"* as they called them, hated the *"heathen Norsemen",* and they quickly departed in boats from Iceland when the Vikings once again invaded their privacy. Some of the Irish Scotties, however, remained to live with the Vikings, and Icelanders today consider themselves by blood-mix, 50% Norwegian, and 50% Irish.

The Vikings of Iceland traded with Norway and Ireland, but developed into an independent country, setting up their own elective legislative and judicial council, which they called, *"The Thing".* The Thing met annually to make rules and to punish those who disobeyed them. By the year 978 A.D., over 5,000 people lived in Iceland, and in that year, the family of Thorvaldson emigrated from Norway. The head of the family was 22 year old Eric, who, because of his rusty colored hair, was known as *"Eric The Red."* Four years after his arrival in Iceland, Eric was called before The Thing. He had killed two of his neighbors during a feud over land rights. The Thing decided that he should be banished from the country for a period of three years. Eric had heard that an Icelandic merchant named Gunbjorn in the year 900 had discovered another land some 200 miles Northwest of Iceland. With his family, two servants and three friends, Eric sailed his 60-foot vessel to this new land, where he decided to wait out his years of exile.

This new land was not all snow and ice as he expected, but along its southern coast and up its fiords, there were green grassy pasturelands, and ten-foot high birch and willow trees. There was also a plentiful supply of fish, wild animals, and seals to eat. He called this new land — *"Greenland."* At the head of a fiord, he built his home of stone and turf, and then proceeded to explore and map the coast. In 986, Eric returned to Iceland, but had no intention of moving back. Instead, he recruited some 750 people to join him in his new *"land of plenty".* A year later, 25 Viking ships, filled with people and provisions, including livestock, sailed for Greenland, but because of stormy weather, eleven of them were either forced to turn back, or sank. Only 480 Icelanders made landfall at Ericsfiord in Southwest Greenland. They built homes, stables and barns, but had to rely on driftwood that they picked up along the shore, as fuel for their new homes. They had planted little, for their summers were short, but lived mostly on hunting seals, walrus, and polar-bears, which they soon began exporting to Iceland and ports in Europe. Products such as seal skins, oil, animal furs, and walrus tusks, were Greenland's main exports, highly cherished by Europeans. Within ten years of Eric's exodus from Iceland, over 2,000 Icelanders lived in Greenland, and a new colony, some 200 miles from Ericsfiord, was settled on Greenland's West Coast. Besides the cold, the only thing these Vikings complained about was the lack of wood to fuel their fires, build their ships, and put adequate roofs on their houses and barns. A few expeditions set out from Greenland to Labrador, some 600 miles to the South, and succeeded in bringing back timber.

The *"Floamanna Saga,"* one of the many ancient handwritten Sagas of Iceland and Norway, mentions that, *"Leif, the 17 year old son of Eric the Red, in year 999 A.D., sailed to Norway with goods from Greenland to trade, without stopping at Iceland on the way there."* This was a 1,800-mile non-stop voyage by a teenaged Viking sea captain, which is the first available record revealing the bold courage and nautical skills of Leif Ericson. He remained that winter in Norway, where King Olaf instructed him in the Gospels of Christ. Norway only a few years earlier had converted from paganism to Christianity. Leif returned home in the Spring, again not stopping at Iceland, intent on spreading the Good News to the Greenland colonists. Leif's mother, Tjodhild, was inspired, and immediately prompted the workmen of

Ericsfiord to build a Catholic church. Eric the Red, however, was not pleased with Christianity, and remained a pagan. His wife then decided not to live in the same house with him, and in that same year the Greenland Thing voted in Cristianity as the national religion. To add to Eric's dilemmas, in the year 1000 A.D., he fell off his horse and was badly injured, contracted a disease, and died in bed four years later. The year 1000 for his son Leif, however, proved to be his most profitable and successful.

In spreading Christianity to the outlying districts of Greenland, Leif visited the home of Bjane Herjulfson who, some 12 years before, in attempting to sail from Iceland to Greenland with his merchant crew, was blown off course in a storm. He told Leif that his ship was driven far to the South. There, he and his men had seen three lands, the first two being full of timber, and the third, rocky. Bjarne said that his crew wanted to go ashore in these lands, but that he refused, for he wanted to get to Greenland, where his father had recently emigrated. He knew by descriptions his father had given him that these forrested lands to the South were not Greenland. This was an exciting revelation to Leif, and he returned to Ericsfiord, where he began organizing an expedition to explore these woodlands.

According to three handwritten Sagas, *"Flatey Book," "Hauksbok,"* and Ari Thorgilson's *"Vinland Norse Saga,"* all written over 100 years after Leif's journey, Leif's eighty-foot sailing *"knorr"* left Greenland with 36 Vikings to explore new worlds to the South. Many historians and archaeologists disagree on just where this voyage took Leif and his crew, but descriptions passed on from word of mouth to the Saga historians, refute conclusions made by some modern day writers that Leif's famed "Vinland," was in Nova Scotia or Newfoundland. Leif's first landfall was a place he called, *"Helluland,"* which in Norse language means, *"land of rocks."* Here the Sagas reveal, *"Leif and his men saw no grass, but only craggy flat rocks between sea and ice. It was barren, with no good qualities."* Some historians believe *"Helluland"* is Labrador, but the Greenland Vikings had already ventured to Labrador many times, and Leif had been there before this southern journey, gathering a cargo of wood. The Vikings already had a name for Labrador — they called it, *"Furdustrand,"* meaning *"land of frost."* Other historians, including noted Norse historian Hjalmar Holand, have concluded that *"Helluland"* is the northern tip of Newfoundland, separated from Labrador by only a few miles of water at the Strait of Belle Isle.

The Vikings continued to sail south and came to a *"flat forested land,"* which Leif called *"Markland,"* meaning *"woodland."* Again, the experts disagree— some say *"Markland"* is Newfoundland, and others believe that the Vikings had arrived at Nova Scotia. The Sagas reveal that the Vikings had to leave this land quickly, for a Nor' easter was coming, and as it is with experienced seamen today, if a well-protected harbor isn't available, it is best to ride out a storm away from the coast. Northeast storms usually last three days. The Sagas read that the Vikings *"sighted land again after two days of sailing in a southwesterly direction."* The Sagas use Roman numerals, and many historians think that the badly written "II" is really a "V", but whichever, sailing southwest, as they were forced to do by the storm, leads them only to New England.

At this third landfall of their voyage, described by them as *"a most beautiful land with wonderful white sand,"* they first landed at an island and *"sipped sweet dew from the grass."* Then they sailed *"through the sound which lay between the island and that cape, which projected northward from the land itself."* They were sailing westward now, and *"at the penninsula's sharp elbow,"* they encountered *"extensive shoals"* and a harbor, where *"at ebb tide, their ship went aground."* The Vikings, however, were so curious to see this new land, that *"they could not wait for high water to float their vessel, and waided ashore. When the tide rose under their vessel, they came back to her and took her up the harbor-river and so into a lake, where they anchored."* Here, Leif decided, they would build *"booths,"* temporary houses, but the Sagas do not mention what material was used to build these houses. There has been much controversy and debate as to where this first American settlement of white men was located. Norse artifacts have been found at Newfoundland, Nova Scotia, Maine, Massachusetts, Rhode Island, and Connecticut. The Norse Sagas descriptions of what Leif saw in this new land, fits many places, but none, I think, more perfectly than Cape Cod, Massachusetts. The island of *"sweet dew,"* could be one of many off the seaward side of the Cape, possibly Nantucket Island. One island has actually disappeared over the centuries off the Cape due to currents and sand erosion. The shoals at the *"elbow"* of the Cape near Monomoy Point, continue to be a dangerous entry to the west for boats, and Bass River, which leads to an inland lake at South Yarmouth, fits the Sagas' descriptions to a T. Also, there is no other distinctive Northern facing cape or penninsula in New England but Cape Cod. This first settlement, however, could have been at Hyannis, Centerville, Chatham, Osterville, Falmouth, or at one of a dozen other places West of the Cape's elbow. The largest lake in the area is *"Chequoquet,"* reached through Centerville Harbor.

Further indication in the Sagas helps us determine that this first Viking settlement in America is Cape Cod, and rules out Newfoundland,

Nova Scotia, and Northern New England as Leif's third landfall. Leif and his men decided to winter over in this land, and in addition to their booths, they erected a large house or hall, probably made of timber, to protect them from the snow and cold which they expected. To their surprise, there was no snow that winter, and say the Sagas, *"the grass withered only a little."* Another curiosity to the Vikings was that, *"the length of day and night in the winter were more nearly equal than in Greenland or Iceland."* It almost goes without saying that anyone staying the winter North of Boston, would see snow, and a lot of it, as would anyone wintering anywhere else in New England, except possibly Cape Cod. At the Cape, a winter without snow has occured a few times even during my lifetime. Because of the Gulf Stream, the seaward side of the Cape is warmer and is often without snow.

The Sagas continue, quoting Leif by saying *"Now I will divide the company into two parts, so that this land can be explored. One half shall remain here with our hall and booths, while the other half goes exploring, but not farther away than they can return in the evening, and they are not to separate."* It was Tyrker the German, Leif's Godfather, who did separate one evening, and did not return with the others to camp. Leif was frightened and furious at the others for loosing Tyrker, and he had everyone search the surrounding woods. *"They had gone only a short way from the hall when Tyrker came to meet them,"* the Sagas record. *"The Southerner,* (as they called Tyrker) *spoke for a long time in his Southern tongue, and rolled his eyes a lot, and made wry faces, but they did not understand what he said. Then he explained in Norse, 'I have found vines and grapes. I was born in the South where neither vines nor grapes are scarce.' Leif said we shall have two tasks then, each day we will either gather grapes and cut vines, or fell timber to make a cargo for my ship."* Tyrker was excited because he now could make wine, which previously the Vikings of Greenland had to import, but he probably was unsuccessful in trying to replant the wild grapevines in Greenland. Wild grapes still grow profusely at Cape Cod, and were a wonder to New England's first English settlers in the 17th century, but wild grapes do not grow in Northern Maine, Nova Scotia, or Newfoundland, which is further indication that Leif Ericson's *"Vinland"* had to be south of those territories.

Two of the 36 crewmen with Leif were *"Haki"* and *"Haekia,"* called *"Gaelic runners"* by the Vikings. They were allowed to explore *"inland of the elbow of the penninsula for three days,"* but encountered no sign of human life. In the Spring, the ship was packed with Vinland goods, mainly timber and grapes, and the Vikings left their camp to return to Greenland. They saw no Indians, or *"Skraelings,"* as they called all *"inferior people,"* until they got to *Helluland,* or what is assumed to be Newfoundland. There they spied five people on an island. The Vikings landed *"and the Skraelings ran,"* two women and a bearded man, *"sank into the ground and disappeared."* Two boy were captured. These were not Indians, but white people who spoke Gaelic, and were understood by Haki and Haekia. The two youths said that, *"our houses are underground, and we are castaways from our people who live across the water."* Then they revealed that they were *"ruled by two kings, Avaladamon and Valdidia, who dressed in white robes"* — This description fits the Irish *Culdee* monks, who when forced out of Iceland, may have setteled in Nova Scotia. The boys were made captive and returned with the Vikings to Greenland as slaves. Marveling at his cargo of timber and grapes, the people of Ericsfiord gave Leif a hero's welcome, and he was henceforth called, *"Leif The Lucky."*

Only a few days after Leif and his crew returned to Greenland in glory, his younger brother, Thorvald, a teenager who also had remarkable navagational skills, criticized Leif for not exploring Vinland further. Leif, according to the Sagas, told him to *"borrow my ship and go exploring Vinland yourself."* Thorvald did just that! With a 30-man crew, including two of Leif's original crewmen, he sailed off to Vinland the following Spring, and easily found the booths and great hall Leif and his men had built the year before. After taking a few days to settle in, Thorvald and his men embarked on an exploration of *"the West Coast of this country."* If they started out from Cape Cod, *"west"* probably means that they sailed towards Rhode Island and Connecticut. However, if their vessel rounded the tip of the Cape first, *"the West Coast"* would mean that they sailed toward Boston and possibly beyond. They saw no Indians during this first exploration voyage, but did locate *"a wooden shed"* on an offshore island, which was probably and Indian corncrib. Thorvald described this coast as *"forested, with many white sand beaches."* At one point in their journey, which apparently lasted only a couple of weeks, they came to a place of *"many bays with small islands."* Fearing that their vessel would go aground, they avoided entering the bays, which could have been either Newport, Boston, or Salem. If they were sailing West, the *place of many bays* could be the Newport area, but if they were exploring *a Western Coast,* the description fits the entrance to Boston. The Vikings returned to Vinland and spent the Fall and Winter there, collecting grapes and hunting wild animals. Thorvald mentions through the Sagas that *"the Winter was very mild."* In the Summer, the Vikings decided to explore again, following the same route they had taken the previous Summer, but only a day or two out, they encountered a storm *"near a cape."* They grounded and broke the ship's large keel. They spent many days on shore, felling trees to build a new keel and fitting it to their ship. Then they placed the old keel *"upright on the headland overlooking the sea, and called the place, 'Keelness'."*

Sailing on, they visited new coastal lands, starting out at the place they had left off the Summer before, *"the place of many bays and islands."* This time they used their small "afterboat" to explore the mouths of the rivers and bays, *"along the North shore."* This last comment of Thorvald's biographer, could mean that they were exploring the coast North of Cape Cod, which would make the place of *"rivers, bays and islands"* either Boston, or Salem, Massachusetts, and *"Keelness"* would then possibly be Provincetown at the tip of Cape Cod. Returning to their ship, they sailed on and approached *"a headland"* which was in *"a fair region."* Thorvald was so impressed with the beauty of this land that he told the crew, *"here is where I will some day build my home."* The water was so deep here that the Vikings were able to bring their 80-foot vessel right into the headland and set a gangplank from the ship to the shore. Some of the crew climbed the headland, and from it, they could see an Indian village inside the mouth of a harbor. Although there are other deepwater headlands leading into harbors in Maine and Massachusetts, the prominent headland at Eastern Point, Cape Ann, overlooking Gloucester Harbor, seems the ideal location as a logical piece to fit this Norse Saga puzzle.

Exploring further on foot, the Vikings came across nine Indians asleep under overturned canoes. Seeing these brawney and bearded white men, wearing helmets and breastplates, carrying shields and strange weapons, must have been a living nightmare to these Indians. They awoke screaming and shouting. The Vikings pounced on them, but there is no record in the Sagas as to which group started the battle. One Indian ran off, but the others stood their ground and fought. They were no match for the broadswords and iron axes. After killing the eight Indians, the Vikings returned to their vessel, raised the gangplank, and anchored offshore. After dark, a fleet of canoes came out of the harbor from the village and surrounded the Viking ship. The Vikings lined their shields along the gunnals of the ship and hid beneath them, to ward off a shower of arrows. This continued until the Indians ran out of arrows, and retreated, paddling back into the harbor. The Viking defense was effective, and only one arrow slipped through the shields, but it struck Thorvald in the armpit. The wound proved fatal, but before he died, Thorvald asked his crew to bury him *"in this pleasant place."* Next morning the Vikings buried him on the headland, placing one cross at his head and another at his feet. The crew then sailed back to Vinland, remained there that Winter, and in the Spring, returned to Greenland.

Eric the Red's third son, Thorstein, was not only saddened by the news of his brother's death, but angry at Thorvald's crew for giving him a Christian burial. Thorstein, like his father, had remained a pagan, and believed that a dead Viking warrior should be placed in an afterboat, set aflame, and shoved off from shore to the open sea, where the god *Odin* awaited to escort his soul to Valhalla. Thorstein organized a crew to return to the coast where his brother was buried, dig him up, and give him a proper pagan sendoff. With his wife Gudrid and a crew of 25, he set sail for Vinland, but a storm swept his ship so far off course, that at one point he caught sight of Ireland. After many weeks at sea the vessel arrived back at Greenland and Thorstein decided to give up the quest. He died a few years later of the black-plague, and Gudrid remarried an Iceland trader named Thorfinn Karlsefni.

According to the *Hauksbok* Sagas, it was Thorfinn Karlsefni who organized the next trip to Vinland, about the year 1010 A.D. His was not just an exploratory and merchant venture however, for he, Gudrid, and 158 other Greenlanders, planned to settle permanently in Vinland. Among them was Freydis, daughter of Eric The Red and half-sister of Leif Ericson, a giantess of enormous strength and of fierce temper. These Viking pioneers headed South in three vessels, loaded with their personal possessions, cattle and other livestock. They easily found *Keelness*, with Thorvald's broken keel still standing on the headland. They then came to a river and sent out runners to explore the woods. They returned with wild grapes and corn. The three Viking vessels were then enveloped in a wild storm and sailed further up the coast to find adequate shelter. They came to another larger river and sailed in for protection. This river had an island at its mouth, surrounded by strong currents, and Karlsefni named the island *"Stumey,"* meaning *"currents."* The Vikings decided to settle, if just for the Winter, at this place. There were marsh grasses here for the cattle to feed on, and birds-eggs so plentiful that, *"you could not walk but to step on one."* Up the river a short way, the Vikings found a small lake, and proceeded to build their houses along its shores. Karlesfni called this first permanent colony of white men on America's soil, *"Straumfiord."* There is good reason to believe, because of Norse artifacts recently found, that *Straumfiord* was in the Kennebec River area, South of Bath, Maine.

It was *"a rough winter, with much snow."* The hunting was poor, and there were no wild grapes to be found in this area. Even in the early Spring, food was scarce, and they subsisted on fish and birds-eggs. A stranded whale, *"of a type never seen before by the Norsemen,"* was killed and consumed by the Viking settlers, but *"it made them all very sick to their stomachs."* One of the Vikings, called Fat Thorhall, who was a poet and wine maker, was disgusted with this new country, especially when he could find no grapes to make his wine. Karlsefni tried to reassure him that they would search further south for grapes in the Summer, but Fat Thorhall, with nine others, decided to return to Greenland. Sailing home in an afterboat, they were blown off course in a storm and landed in Ireland. The ten of them were captured and made slaves by *"wild Irishmen,"* and Fat Thorhall died in captivity.

In the summer of 1011 A.D., hoping to find a more pleasant place to settle, the Vikings packed their belongings and livestock aboard the three ships and sailed South. *"They voyaged a long way,"* the Sagas reveal, *"until they reached a river running through a lake to the ocean. Only at high water could their vessel get into this river."* Although this was not Leif Ericson's Vinland, and may have been further South, possibly Newport, Rhode Island, wild grapes were found here, *"on higher ground near the lake."* The surrounding forest had many wild animals to hunt and trap, and the lake and surrounding sea provided plenty of fish. They dug ditches at low tide along the coast, and when the tide came in and then out again, they would hand-catch flat fish (flounders) in the ditch. The Vikings decided to resettle here, and they built homes around the lake. Karlsefni named the place, *"Hop"* which some historians believe means, *"hope."* The first Winter at *"Hop"* was mild and the cattle could be left outdoors.

In the Spring, one morning the Vikings saw many canoes, *"like charcoal scattered on the surface of the water,"* coming from the South around the headland and heading for the new Viking village. The Viking men lifted their white shields in friendship and many Indians landed, wanting to trade. They bartered furs and animal skins for red cloth and trinkets. The Indians wanted Viking spears, swords, and axes, but Karlsefni refused to give up weapons in trade. Instead, he offered them milk and cheese, which they had never tasted before. The Indians especially liked the *"sweet wine water"* of the cows, but when a bull came snorting out of the woods, it frightened them so that they ran back to their canoes and paddled off. Karlsefni described the Indians as *"ugly and dark, with broad cheeck-bones and coarse hair."* He knew that despite their fear of the bull, they would be back some day to barter for the milk they loved so well.

"Karlsefni let make a stronge fence of pales around his abode and made all ready there," says the *Flatey Book.* This fence was all but completed when the Indians returned, in lesser number than before.

They again traded furs and skins for milk and cloth, but during this bartering session, an Indian tried to steal an iron-headed axe from a Viking. In an attempt to get it back, the Indian struggled with the axe owner and the handle of the axe broke. The Viking then killed the Indian. The other Indians quickly retreated to their canoes and again paddled away in fear. Three weeks later, hundreds of canoes carrying armed Indians appeared offshore. *"The Skraelings were all uttering loud cries, and they sprang from their boats,"* the *Hauksbok* relates. *"They met the Norsemen and they fought together."* The Indians fought with stone-axes and slings made of hide that projected rocks with great accuracy. *"In the midst of a fierce shower of missiles,"* Karlsefni saw the Indians using a strange weapon: *"They lifted up on a pole a black round object, the size of a sheep's belly, and let if fly, making a terrible noise when it hit the ground."* Although it didn't seem to do any damage, the sound of it so frightened the Vikings *"that they fled the settlement by the lake and ran up the side of the river."* The Indians followed in hot pursuit.

"Why are you running from wretches like these?" shouted Freydis, daughter of Eric The Red. The men didn't listen to her, but retreated to an overhanging cliff by the river, where they were cornered by Indians on every side. *"Freydis saw a dead Norseman in front of her, his sword laying beside him. Freydis took it and prepared to defend herself. She let fall her shift and slapped her breasts with the sword."* Seeing the enraged nude giantess before them, slapping her enormous breast with the broad end of the sword, stopped the advancing Indians in their tracks. The Indians, it is assumed, feared demented people. Indian superstitions, revealed later in history, conclude that they believed the insane were the Great Spirit's chosen people. No doubt they considered Freydis to be a mad woman, for they mumbled among themselves and then ran back to their canoes and paddled away as fast as they could. Freydis was the heroine of Hop and *"Karlsefni praised her courage."* In the battle, four Indians were killed and two Vikings, but some thirty Vikings were wounded.

The survivors feared that the Indians would return, so once again, they hauled their belongings and livestock aboard the vessels and sailed off, returning to Straumfiord. In the Autumn, Karlsefni and a few men explored the coast North of Straumfiord, but returned before the winter to be on hand when Gudrid gave birth to his first child. They called him *"Snorri."* Snorri Karlsefni, therefore, was the first recorded white child to be born in the Americas. After an especially harsh winter, the Vikings once again loaded their ships, but this time they headed back home to Greenland. At Markland, where they camped out for a few months, one of their vessels was lost, and some of the passengers drowned, but two vessels made it to Ericsfiord without further incident. In a geography book, written in 1075 A.D. by Adam of Bremen in Germany, he states that, *"Vinland was discovered by many people."* The book also mentions that Thorfinn Karlsefni *"went from Greenland to Norway with the richest cargo that ever sailed from Greenland."*

The final Norse Saga concerning Vinland is about Freydis, the heroine of Hop. A few years after she returned to Greenland with the others in Karlsefni's party, she organized an expedition to Vinland herself. She, with the help of two Greenland brothers, Helgi and Finnbogi, intended to make Vinland a permanent tradingpost. Helgi and Finnbogi, with a crew of twenty, arrived at Vinland before Freydis and her crew of equal number arrived. The brothers were living in Leif's large hall, and when Freydis arrived, she kicked them out so she could live there. The brothers then *"made themselves a hall away from the sea near a lake, but not far from Leif's hall."* There was animosity between Freydis and the brothers right from the start. As the two crews *"collected grapes, mosur wood, and timber,"* further feuding developed. Freydis ended the arguements by killing the two brothers. Then she had her crew kill the competing crew. She further rid herself of the other five women in Vinland, by lining them up outside Leif's hall and chopping off their heads with a battle-axe. Freydis then had her crew load the vessels, and skippering one of them herself, delivered the cargo of timber and grapes to Iceland, some 2,500 miles away. She remained in Iceland for the rest of her life.

In the year 1341, some 325 years later, the Roman Catholic Church sent a Norwegian priest named Ivar Bardson to Greenland to be the Bishop of that country. He was told that an estimated 9,000 people lived in Greenland's two colonies, but when he arrived, no one was there. The houses, barns and churches were still standing, and a few chickens, cows and sheep were running wild in the western colony, but there were no other signs of life. Many historians believe that the Greenlanders either all died of the black-plague, or were attacked and killed by Eskimoes. Some believe that the Vikings intermarried with the Eskimoes and adopted a nomadic life. Another theory is that the Vikings emigrated en-masse to Vinland, and there, over some 300 years, took on Indian ways and appearances. Bishop Bardson in his summary to the Pope and the Bishops of Norway concludes: *"The Greenlanders gave up Christianity, renounced their virtues and turned to the people of Vinland."*

II
THE FUGARWEE MYSTERY

One problem with American history is that until about 370 years ago no European visiting our shores knew where he was. Christopher Columbus, to his dying day, never realized that he had found and explored the Americas, but was convinced he had discovered a new route to the outer islands of the East Indies. John Cabot, who arrived at Newfoundland from England, five years later in 1497, swore that he had landed in China. The following year, King Henry VIII of England fitted out five vessels and gave Cabot 200 men to *"explore further West and find Japan,"* and although one leaky ship turned back and returned to Bristol, the others disappeared somewhere off the Americas. The Danes and Portugese, in a joint venture under Joao Corte Real, landed presumably in Newfoundland some 20 years before Cabot, but readily admitted they didn't know where they were.

Even the New England Indians, who had been here presumably for some 12,000 years, gave names difficult to pronounce to the places they lived, and they were constantly changing these names. If an unusual incident or decisive battle took place in a certain area, the local tribal chief would give that place a new name, but a neighboring tribe would often ignore the name change, or was unaware of it, and continued calling it by its old name. The Indians were also continuously changing their own names. An Indian boy was given one name, but when he became a warrior at age 15, he was given another, and if he later performed some courageous feat, he was renamed again. To add to this confusion, experienced by our first explorers, traders and settlers, New England was divided into Indian nations, which were further divided into tribes and then into almost 100 sub-tribes, but one tribe often called another tribe by a name other than the name they gave themselves. Our Pilgrim and Puritan forefathers helped to solve this problem by killing off or exporting most of the New England Indians, and by giving vast territories Indian names, such as, Massachusetts and Connecticut — with few people living then or now, knowing what these names mean.

Many American history books that we read as school children because of England's influence on us, credit Englishmen as making first contacts with the North American Indians on or about the turn of the 17th century, and John Smith is often acclaimed as New England's first explorer. Smith explored and surveyed the coast in 1614, of what was then known as *"North Virginia,"* and gave "New England" its name. First contact with the *"Beothuck"* Indians of Newfoundland and the

"Micmacs" of Nova Scotia, was made by French *"Breton"* and Spanish *"Basque"* fishermen at about the turn of the 16th century. In 1508, a French captain named Aubert captured three of the *"Beothucks"* and shipped them back to Paris for display, as Cabot had done in 1497. Marquis de La Roche, a Breton nobleman, attempted to colonize Cape Sable, Nova Scotia with French convicts in 1598, and mentions in his report to the King of France that, *"the Portuguese have had cows at pasture here for sixty years"* — meaning that there was a European Settlement of some sort only 120 miles from New England, as early as the year 1538. In the year 1577, Sir Humphrey Gilbert, with a ship-load of Englishmen, sailed down the coast of Maine and traded with the *"Penobscot"* Indians, and reported when he got back to England that the French were already trading with the Maine Indians, *"defrauding them and feeding them strong drink."* Six years later, Etienne Belanger, trading for France, *"went ashore twelve places"* in Maine, exchanging trinkets for furs with the Indians.

The first European we know of who sailed up the New England coast, was Giovanni de Verrazano, in 1524, ninety years before John Smith sailed down the coast. Like Columbus and Cabot before him, Verrazano was an Italian working for another country. He was exploring for Frances I of France, and his crew was made up of Frenchmen. His first stop in New England was at Newport, Rhode Island, but he called it *"Refugio."* Here, he tells us, *"we spent many days with the natives, who were friendly and generous, beautiful and civilized. They excel us in size, and are of a bronze color, some inclining more to whiteness and others of tawny color. Their faces are sharply cut, and there were among them two kings of so goodly stature and shape, as is possible to declare, the eldest being forty years of age. Upon his naked body he wore an animal skin, and his hair was tied up behind with various knots. About his neck he wore a large chain garnished with stones of different colors. The women are very handsome and fair. Some wear very rich skins of the lynx. Their hair is adorned with ornaments and hangs down before on both sides of their breasts. We saw many of the men wearing breast-plates wrought of copper."* Their village, Verrazano described as *"small, surrounded by cultivated fields,"* in which they grew corn, peas, squash and pumpkins, *"and their homes are made of saplings covered with reed mats."*

Only at Newport did Verrazano and his men meet *"fair-skinned"* Indians. At Maine, which he named *"Fremont,"* the Indians were dark and less civilized. *"When we went ashore,"* he wrote in his report to the King, *"they shot at us with their bows, making great outcries, and afterwards fled into the woods. When we departed from them they showed all signs of discourtesy and disdain, as was possible for any creature to invent. They were clad in skins and furs, but had no grain or any kind of tillage."* Verrazano sailed on to Nova Scotia, and gave the famous fishing port, *"Cape Breton"* its name, which indicates how entrenched the Celtic Bretons of France were in Nova Scotia in 1524.

The most remarkable discovery by Verrazano, but not mentioned in his Journal, probably for the sake of secrecy, was the discovery of "a tall stone Norman Villa" at Newport, Rhode Island. It was a man-made tower, like those built by the Vikings in Normandy and in Norway in about the year 1300 A.D. He described it to the King as *"round with eight pillars supporting eight arches."* It had two floors, with a lookout tower facing out to sea. In Normandy similiar towers had four purposes–as living quarters, a defense fortress, a church, and a lighthouse. A fireplace on the second floor, facing an open window that overlooked the sea at Newport, had to be a constant nightly beacon. The *"Viking Tower of Newport"* as it is called today, still stands in the downtown area.

Deeply cut into the stones inside the tower, are runic inscriptions of the ancient cryptic Norse language, but these weren't discovered until 1946, by two visiting Norwegian archaeologists. According to ancient Viking law, only a specially chosen pagan priest could be a Rune-Master, and only he could chisel messages into the rocks and decipher rune inscriptions left by another Rune-Master. Even after the Norsemen adopted Christianity, only a Catholic Priest could be a Rune-Master, and in Iceland, up until the 17th century, anyone other than a Rune-Master who attempted to decipher the message on a runestone, was executed. One of the runes in the Newport Tower is thought to read, *"the seat,"* possibly meaning that this was the seat of the church in this new land. *"Rune Monk,"* is carved onto another stone inside the tower. The runic word *"Hnakr,"* is thought by some to stand for the name *"Henricus,"* who, medievil scriptures inform us, was *"the Norwegian Bishop of Greenland and Vinland"* about the year 1123 A.D. The first Bishop of *"Greenland and Vinland under Pope Pashal II, in 1112 A.D.,"* Vatican records in Rome reveal, was Norwegian *"Erik Gnupsson"* — indicating that the Catholic Church considered Vinland to be well populated with Christian Vikings at that time. Some historians believe Gnupsson and Henricus were the same person.

Bishop Henricus' popularity peaked again in 1965, when Yale University published a controversial medievil world map, showing Vinland as a separate continent West of Ireland. A caption on the supposedly long-lost map mentions *"the second journey to Vinland by*

Henricus," about 120 years after Leif Ericson's discovery. Although some historians question the authenticity of the map, Henricus, the *"Vinland Rune-Monk."* was in the headlines again in 1971. A carpenter from Quincy, Massachusetts, Walter Elliott, who spent his spare time hunting the wilderness of Maine for Indian artifacts, stumbled across five carved stones buried along the banks of Spirit Pond, west of the Kennebec River. Not understanding what the markings on them meant, he brought the stones to the Peabody Museum at Harvard University. The 6 to 8-inch stones had many runes deeply etched into them. One read, *"Vin 1010,"* another read *"Hoob,"* thought to mean *"Hop,"* the name of Thorfin Karlsefni's Viking colony. One was deciphered to mean *"Henricus in October, 1123 A.D."* Another depicted a crude map, which is thought to be a map of the surrounding area of Spirit Pond, with an arrow pointing down what is now the Morse River and aiming toward the tip of Cape Cod, and under it, the name *"Vinland."* The runestone that mentions Henricus goes on to say, *"he sailed sixty-eight days, South thirty-four days and back thirty-four days,"* which suggests that the Bishop explored a good deal of the American coast, and possibly into the Gulf of Mexico. One blue colored stone reads *"Miltiaki,"* which in the old Norse language means, *"as seen by me,"* and below it are sketches of a fish, bird, deer, snake, Indian face, a stick-Indian rowing a canoe, a bow and arrow, and a drying animal skin, with a chisled runic signature on the bottom, *"The Rune Monk."* The text of one of the *"Spirit Pond Stones"* was so worn that experts could not attempt to translate what was written on it, but the discovery of these runestones, along with the runes found in Newport's Viking Tower, left little doubt in any historian's mind that the Norsemen had been here in New England.

Further North up the Atlantic coast at Cutler, Maine, the remains of what is thought to be the foundation of Viking buildings and a dam were discovered at Norse Pond, but archaeologists have yet to dig the site. One wonders, however, why Maine's early settlers decided to name this small body of water, *"Norse Pond"?* At Sebec Lake near Greeley's Landing in Maine, a small runestone was recently uncovered, that reads, *"Auth Rekr,"* thought to mean, *"you will find good luck if you drift further along."* This area near the Penobscot River is noted for its good hunting and fishing, so we might assume that this is what the Rune-Master meant. A runestone was found in a burial mound at Ellsworth, Maine in 1897, which read, *"Sthanar Raith,"* possibly meaning *"Steinar,"* which is an old Norse family name, and *"Raith"* meaning, *"here ruled."* At nearby Bar Harbor, an old Norse penny, dating back to 1068 A.D., was uncovered during an Indian mound excavation in 1957. The coin depicts a rooster's head on one side and a Norse cross within a circle on the other. It has been deemed authentic by experts at the National Museum of Norway, as has a Viking spoon of the same era, found on a beach at New London, Connecticut. It is now on display at the Danish Museum, Denmark. Across some sixty miles of ocean from Ellsworth and the Bar Harbor area, a runestone was discovered at Yarmouth, Nova Scotia, which reads *"Leivur Eriku Resr,"* meaning *"Leif to Erik, raises this monument."* Also at nearby Tor Bay, Nova Scotia, a Viking battle-axe head was uncovered by a farmer while plowing his field. On it is the inscription, *"for divine protection."* A similar battle-axe was found at Rocky Nook near Plymouth, Massachusetts. One is now on display at Connecticut's Wordsworth Athenaeum and the other at Howland House in Plymouth.

At Martha's Vineyard, off the coast of Cape Cod, a six-foot rock at Oak Bluffs, was said to have a runic inscription on it, visible to sailors plying Nantucket Sound. The rock, however, tumbled from its perch and landed on a beach, face up, and by the early 1900s, storms and sand erosion placed it permanently underwater. A similar seaward facing boulder was discovered at Noman's Land, a tiny island three miles south of Martha's Vineyard, in 1926. The runes on the boulder were said to read, *"Leif Erikson's Island - Thirty Men."* Some thought the carvings in the rock were a hoax — the boulder disappeared into the sea, victim of the 1938 hurricane. Seven other large boulders with what appear to be runic markings on them, were discovered along the banks of the Merrimack River, at Newbury and Byfield in the early 1900s. Jim Whittall, noted archaeologist and founder of the Early Sites Research Society in Rowley, Massachusetts, say that, *"the writing on the Byfield Stones is not runic, but on some of them, it might be ogham,"* which is an ancient Celtic language. Mystery Hill, an ancient site of rock settlement ruins, some forty miles up the Merrimack River at Salem, New Hampshire, was once thought to be the remains of a Norse settlement, but is now believed to be Celtic, and possibly a village built by Irish Culdee monks. Probably the most controverial writings or markings found on a boulder, are those carved into a forty-ton rock located on the banks of the Taunton River at Dighton, Massachusetts, eight miles North of Fall River. Dighton Rock was discovered by New England's first settlers, and even then, was considered a marvel, with various speculations as to who might have carved the messages in the stone. In 1837, foremost Danish antiquarian, Carl Christian Rafn, with noted Icelandic historian, Finn Magnusen, after studying the rock inscriptions, concluded that the carvings were Viking runes. They deciphered one message on the rock to read, *"Thorfinn and his 151 companions took possession of this land."* They also said that one rune was so worn that they couldn't read or decipher it, but thought that the Roman numerals in it, *"CXXXI,"* stood for the year *"1131,"* which was about the time Bishop Henricus was sailing around, leaving messages everywhere. The Massachusetts government preserved Dighton Rock in 1974 by erecting a building around it, and enshrining it as a Commonwealth treasure.

The locations of these Viking remnants help define where in New England these ancient Norsemen explored and settled, and also introduce a strange unexplainable coincidence into American history; it seems that New England's 17th century explorers were unknowingly attracted to the very same spots the Vikings were. The Gosnold settlers of 1602, chose an island less than four miles from Noman's Land, seven miles from Martha's Vineyard, 17 miles from Newport's Viking Tower, and less than 17 miles from Cape Cod's elbow, where Leif Ericson possibly built his *"booths."* The 1607 English settlement at a village in Maine called *"Sagadahoc"* was on the Kennebec River, less than two miles from Spirit Pond, where the Vikings' *"Straumfiord"* was probably located. It was also some eight miles from Damariscove Island, where French fishermen settled in 1614. English fishermen settled at Cape Ann in 1617, where some historians believe Thorvald, Leif's brother, was put to rest, and Provincetown, where the Mayflower made first landfall in 1620, may well have been Thorvald's *"Keelness."* It was near here, with the Mayflower anchored off Provincetown at the tip of Cape Cod, the Pilgrims dug into an Indian mound, hoping to find dried corn that the Indians had stored for the winter. Instead, they uncovered the graves of a man and a boy. The body of the man had, *"fine yellow hair still on it, and some of the flesh unconsumed,"* writes Plymouth Governor Bradford. The body was wrapped in canvas and was wearing a pair of pants. Buried with him were *"fine white beads, needles, bowls, three old iron things, and a knife."* This obviously was not the grave of an Indian, but who this blonde man was remains a mystery. Also, Provincetown's first settlers in 1670, uncovered a large stone wall buried in the sand, while digging cellar holes for their homes.

Another unsolved mystery concerning the Norsemen in New England, which perplexed our first explorers was, where is *"Norumbega"*? It first started appearing on world maps in 1527, and it was always placed by the European mapmakers somewhere close to, but South of Cape Breton, Nova Scotia. On some maps, Norumbega was but a pinpoint on the usually inaccurate outline of America's East Coast, but on other maps, Norumbega was designated as covering hundreds of miles. The mapmaker Hieronemus Verrazano, brother of the explorer, placed Norumbega north of the *"Norman Villa"* his brother had discovered in 1524. The greatest mapmaker of the day, Gerard Mercator, placed Norumbega south of a great cape, thought to be Cape Cod, in his 1540 to 1555 maps. Nobody knew where Norumbega was or how it got its name, but old Breton fishermen said *"it was a great city of towering stone buildings, where the natives wore gold ornaments, and was located at the Y of a wide river, just South of a cape."* Every explorer who left Europe for America in the 1500s and early 1600s was more anxious to find Norumbega than he was to locate a Northwest passage through the Americas to Asia. Many writers and historians have assumed that *"Norumbega"* was just another name for *"Vinland,"* and may have stood for *"New Norway."* Norway itself was displayed on the maps of the 16th century, as *"Norvegia,"* and so the name probably originated with the Vikings.

There were many fascinating tales of Norumbega, told by traders, fishermen and sailors, circulating through the cities of Europe. After a long voyage up the American coast in 1524, Etienne Gomez returned to Spain and declared that he had found Norumbega. It was a wide river with many islands at its mouth, near a cape, with an Indian village at a fork where the river branched out in two directions, but the natives were not clad in gold, and there were no tall stone buildings. Gomez was apparently some 400 years too early to see "gold and tall buildings," for many historians believe that he had sailed into New York Harbor.

About fifty years later, a pamphlet on adventures in Norumbega by sailor David Ingram was being devoured by wide-eyed readers in London and in every English hamlet. Ingram, with more than 100 other English seamen, had been *"marooned"* at Tampico, Mexico by privateersman Sir John Hawkins in 1568, after his vessel had been crippled by the Spanish. Ingram with some of the others decided to head Northeast in hopes of finding a fisherman or trader that would give them a ride back home to England. They walked and paddled canoes with the help of the Indians, all the way to the Gulf of St. Lawrence, where they met French Captain Campaigne who was trading for furs. He gave the three sole survivors of the long trek, Ingram, John Twine and Bob Brown, a lift back to England in his ship the Gargoyle. Although Ingram's lengthy pamphlet on his two years of travel through America was filled with exaggerations, the English were craving information on life in the New World and believed every word. *"I have been to Norumbega,"* he wrote, *"which is a town half a mile long, and hath many streets, far broader than any streets in London. The men there go naked, saving only the middle part of them is covered with skin of beasts and with leafs. On their arms, they wear hoops of gold and silver, which are a good thickness, and the women go appareled with plates of gold over their body, much like unto armour. About the middest of their bodies, they wear leafs...*" He also mentions that, "*there is a tree there, that when its leafs are pressed, produces a pleasant drink as good as any kind of wine,*" — possibly Ingram had been to Norumbega, mistaking copper for gold, and for the first time, drank the juice of wild grapes. English Captain John Walker hired Ingram as his pilot to sail to Norumbega in 1579. Somewhere in New England, Ingram directed the ship up a river that had a wide entrance, peppered with a few islands, but the Indian village at the Y of this river, they found deserted. They did find some furs and hides inside the wigwams and stole them. Upon their return to England, Walker announced that, "*we did discover a silver mine within the River of Norumbega, on the North Shore, upon a hill not far from the riverside, about six leagues from the mouth thereof,*" but he would not divulge to anyone where Norumbega was. England's John Rut had searched for it as early as 1528, and Jean Alfonse of France had sailed from Cape Breton to Florida in 1541, in search of the elusive Norumbega.

Into the 17th century, the French and English explorers and traders competed to be first to Norumbega. Spain was reaping rewards of gold and silver from Central and South America, and the French and English were jealous. The tall tales of "*a glorious city of gold*" somewhere in New England had reached fever pitch, and men like England's Bartholomew Gosnold and Samuel de Champlain of France were obsessed with finding Norumbega. Gosnold left Falmouth, England, in the small bark Concord with 32 crewmen, on March 6, 1602. He first made landfall at what is now Kennebunkport, Maine and sailed South. At Portsmouth, New Hampshire, the Concord was greeted by a French shallop being sailed by six Indians. They used "*an iron grapple*" to attach their shallop to the English ship, and "*came boldly aboard us... One savage wore a waistcoat, breeches, stockings, shoes and a hat. Another had breeches of blue cloth,*" obviously European made. "*All the others were naked,*" wrote crewman Gabriel Archer. In their sailboat was "*a copper kettle,*" Archer noticed, "*and they spoke Christian words.*" It was also evident to these New England explorers, as it was to the first French missionaries in Nova Scotia, that the Indian-"*Algonkian*" language was sprinkled with Gaelic and Norse words. Asked about their French boat and European clothes, the Indians indicated that French and Basque fisherman had visited them often, trading trinkets for furs and hides. These New Hampshire Indians were, "*of tall stature, with black swarthy complexions, but their eyebrows were painted white,*" reported Archer.

Sailing on and rounding Cape Cod, the Concord came to Noman's Island, where the crew went ashore. They left that island, which Gosnold named *"Martha's Vinyard,"* and sailed to the island that we call today Martha's Vineyard. Gosnold named it *"Dover Cliff,"* obviously because of the colorful clay cliffs at Gay Head on the Vineyard. Also, *"because we had pestered our ship so with codfish,"* wrote Archer, *"we decided to call this place Cape Cod."* They then sailed the length of the Elizabeth Islands, also named by Gosnold, but not for the Queen. He named them for his sister, and decided to camp on the last of the chain, known today as Cuttyhunk Island. There the explorers found a fresh water pond near the sea, with a small island in the middle. Here they built a tradingpost of timber, and a flat-bottomed boat to go to and from the tiny island. Gosnold realized that the mainland with a wide-mouthed harbor was only eight miles away, and the area fit all the descriptions of Norumbega. What he didn't realize was that if he hadn't stopped at Cuttyhunk and had kept on sailing for 17 more miles, he would have come to Verrazano's *"Refugio"* and the Norse Tower.

On their sixth day at the island, they saw three Indians land in a canoe. When the Indians saw the bearded white-men they panicked and ran into the woods. Gosnold then stole their canoe, and eventually brought it with him back to England. The next day, Gosnold and his crew sailed to the mainland, to what would be the Westport-New Bedford area of today. Hundreds of Indians came to meet them when they landed. *"They were olive skinned with dark hair,"* Gosnold reported, *"and they were armed with bows and arrows. They wore deerskins and are of tall stature. Their Indian pipes were steeled with copper, and one wore a copper breast-plate. They were exceedingly courteous, gentle of disposition, and well conditioned, exceeding all others we have seen in shape and looks."* Archer reported that, *"the men, women and children, entertained the Captain, giving him many furs, tobacco, turtles, hemp, chains, and such things."* Gosnold gave their chief, *"a straw hat and two knives,"* but the chief didn't like the straw hat and gave it away. Another Concord crewman, John Brereton, wrote of the meeting that, *"the Indians have a great store in copper,"* which Brereton mistook at first for gold. *"Some of the copper is very red and some of a paler color, none of them but have chains, earrings, or collars of this metal."* He also noticed that every Indian carried his own matches: *"Everyone carrieth about him a purse of tewed leather, a mineral stone and a flat emery stone, tied fast to the end of a little stick. Gently he striketh upon the mineral stone, and within a strike or two, a spark falleth upon a piece of touchwood, and with the least spark, he maketh the fire."*

The Indians paddled out from the mainland in great numbers many times to the tradingpost at Cuttyhunk. *"They ate many meals with us,"* wrote Archer, *"loving our food, except for our mustard, whereat they made a sour face."* The Indians also helped the Concord crew to pick sassafras on the island and load it aboard the vessel. The English considered sassafras a cure for pox, plague and syphilis. The crewmen found the Indians to be hard workers, playful, and often quite humorous. They seemed to enjoy mimicking the English, as they did the noises of the birds and animals in the woods, and became so proficient at it, that they could repeat long sentences, sounding genuinely English. They also made beards like the Englishmen wore *"out of animal hairs,"* and since Indians are unable to grow facial hair, they wore the imitation beards to delight the crew. The Englishmen also noted that the Indians were sometimes sneak-thieves, and would pick up and keep tools or objects left lying about in the tradingpost or aboard the Concord. Maybe this was merely another way the Indians decided to imitate the English, for Captain Gosnold had stolen their canoe before he noted that *"the Indians are such thieves."*

In England, before the Concord expedition began, more than half of the crewmen had agreed to stay in America and live the winter, while Gosnold returned to England with his cargo and come back for them in the Spring, but an incident a few days before the Concord was about to depart from Cuttyhunk changed their minds. Two of the crew, while in the woods foraging for food and sassafras, were attacked by four Indians. One of the crewmen was struck in the leg with an arrow, but the other crewman, *"a stout fellow,"* wrestled all four Indians to the ground, and cut their bow-strings with his knife. The Indians ran off, and the crewmen returned to the tradingpost. With hostile Indians about, no crew member would remain at the tradingpost through the winter, and in mid-July, 1602, all 33 Englishmen returned on the Concord to their homeland, and they never returned. It is interesting to note, however, that Gosnold learned from the Indians that their name for Cuttyhunk Island was *"Poochutohunkunnoh,"* meaning in Algonkian, *"the place of departure,"* but one wonders whose departure, and to where?

The following Spring two vessels, the Speedwell and the Discoverer, left England for New England with 48 men under the command of Captain Martin Pringe. Items aboard the vessel to be used in trade with the Indians were: shoes, stockings, saws, shovels, hatchets, knives, beads, bugles, mirrors, and needles, and to build a new tradingpost-fort in the New World, they brought hammers and nails. Their first landfall was Cape Cod, *"where we found cod, better than those in New-*

foundland," commented Pringe. *"Departing hence, we bore into the great Gulf which Captain Gosnold over-shot the year before,"* he wrote, *"and coasting, we found people on the North side thereof."* The ships were anchored and the crews went ashore, at what is now, we assume, either Barnstable, Sandwich, Wellfleet or Plymouth, Massachusetts. *"We were approached by over one hundred and twenty savages, and we gave them peas and beans to eat."* Pringe and his men remained at, what he called, *"Whitson's Bay"* for seven weeks. For the first weeks, the Indians and Englishmen enjoyed each other's company, *"a boy in our company playing gitterne* (guitar), *and the Indians taking great delight in it, dancing in a ring and singing."* The Indians here, Pringe described, were much like those that greeted Gosnold the year before; *"somewhat taller than we, strong and swift, wearing feathers in their knotted hair, and aprons of leather and bear skin, like an Irish mantle, over one shoulder. A few were wearing plates of brass a foot long and a half a foot broad before their breasts."* Pringe was interested in the Indian gardens of *"tobacco, cucumbers, maiz* (corn), *pumpions* (pumpkins), *and such."* He even planted a few crops himself and was surprised to see his garden begin to sprout before he departed. His main interest, however, was furs and sassafras. He had his crews in the surrounding woods collecting both, but one day, in the seventh week, while the sassafras crew was napping in the woods, *"there came down seven score savages, armed with six-foot bows and arrows. They enviorned the house we had built on shore wherin were four of our men, alone with their muskets."* On the Speedwell, seeing Indians *"harrassing our guards, we caused a piece ordinance* (ship's cannon) *to be shot off, to give terror to the Indians and to warn our men in the woods."* Pringe had two dogs with him which all the Indians feared, and he called on them to chase the Indians away from the guards who had barracaded themselves in the makeshift house. *"The dogs and a second shot from the cannon, sent the Indians fleeing,"* but Pringe decided he had overstayed his welcome. The day before the ships set sail for Maine, the Indians set the woods on fire, and 200 Indians came to the beach. *"Some came to us in boats, urging us to come back,"* said Pringe, but he kept going, sailing all the way to the Kennebec River, where he and his men built a fort, which they hoped would also someday be a tradingpost. As much as Pringe liked the South Shore of Massachusetts, he thought the skins and furs of Maine were of better quality, and the animals more abundant.

In the Spring of 1605, England's Commander of Plymouth Port, Sir Ferinando Gorges, sponsor of the previous two expeditions to New England, sent out a third in the ship Archangel, under command of George Waymouth. The mission, however, was not angelic; Sir Gorges wanted to know where the golden city of Norumbega was. To find out, he ordered Waymouth to bring back savages to England, where he intended to teach them English and to grill them in hopes of uncovering the whereabouts of their mysterious city. First arriving at Martha's Vineyard, where he met a storm, Waymouth sailed to Maine and up the Kennebec River to Pringe's St. George's Fort. Crewman James Rofier reports that *"when we came on shore, the Indians most kindly entertained us, taking us by the hand and bringing us to sit down by their fire; they filled their pipes and gave us of their excellent tobacco."* Rofier said that, *"their bodies were painted with black, and their faces, some with red, some with black and some with blue."* The Indians were invited to sleep aboard the Archangel, *"but they wouldn't stay on the ship unless one of the crew stayed on shore to sleep with their people... One of them, being suspicious, withdrew himself into the woods. Two others came to receive a platter of peas, which meat they love... We used little delay but suddenly laid hands upon them and it was much as six of us could do to get them into the boat; for they were strong, and so naked as our best hold was by their long hair."* By this means, Waymouth and his crew kidnapped five Indians and returned to England, turning some of them over to Sir Gorges, and one to John Popham, England's Lord Chief Justice. Wrote Sir Gorges, *"they have great civility of manners, far from the rudeness of our common people. They are objects of great wonder and crowds follow them on the streets. I only wanted information, and have no intention of making them slaves."* Sir Gorges kept three of them in England for two years, teaching them English, and gaining invaluable information from them, but none of them it seems had heard of Norumbega. One of them was a *"Sagamore,"* a personal councilor to one of Maine's tribal chiefs, whose name was *"Tahanedo."* He told Sir Gorges that the Indians called the area of Maine, *"Mawooshen,"* and it was where the *"Abenaki"* tribe of the *"Tarentine"* nation lived. The *Abenakis,* unlike the tribes to the South, in what is now New Hampshire and Massachusetts, were nomadic and did not grow crops. They lived by hunting and fishing.

Sir Gorges sent two of the Anglicized Indians, *"Mannido"* and *"Assacomet"* back to America aboard his ship Richard, captained by Henry Challons, but they were captured by Spaniards off the Virginia coast, and Challons, his crew, and the two Maine Indians ended up in a Spanish prison. The following year, 1607, two more of the Indian captives were shipped back home in the ships Gift and Mary & John, with 65 English men and women who planned to settle permanently in New England. Their leaders were Captains George Popham and Raleigh

Gilbert, two men who disliked each other. So, this first settlement of Pilgrims in America, sponsored by England's Plymouth Company, was doomed from the start. They built their villages down river in the Kennebec, below Pringe's Fort St. George, not far from Spirit Pond, where the Viking runestones were later found. Yet, today, the remains of their *"plantation,"* which they called *"Sagadahoc"* have not been found.

One of the settlers, Thomas Hanham, reported that 2,930 Abenaki Indians lived nearby. They were *"bold and curious"* of these new white settlers, and they, *"cautious and suspicious"* of the Indians, but it wasn't the Indians that caused these English pioneers to finally disband. Like the Viking settlers of *"Straumsfiord"* some 600 years before them, it was mainly the harsh Maine winter that defeated them. By Spring of 1608, only 20 of the original 65 were still living at *Sagadahoc.* A few had given up in December and returned to England on the Gift, which was forced to stop at the Azores to sell their timber and cannon for food. Many left behind, including leader George Popham, died from starvation and exposure to cold weather. Not willing to spend another Winter in Maine, the survivors packed up their belongings and returned to England on September 30, 1608 — their brave venture lasting some 15 months. Their reports of ice, snow, and brutal cold in New England, disuaded many others who were planning to settle here in the early 17th century.

Sir Gorges was obviously disappointed at the failure of his Sagadahoc venture, even though Thomas Hanham reported to him that, *"some oare was found in this Tarentine Country that did prove to be silver."* Gorges wanted the gold of Norumbega, but kept his expeditions going with the sale of timber and fish, and from money gained in the highly profitable beaver-fur trade. Three years after the Sagadahoc misadventure, Captain Edward Harlow sailed across the Atlantic to capture more Indians in New England. At Monhegan Island, Maine, he kidnapped three, but one named *"Pechmo,"* managed to jump ship. He returned a few nights later and attacked Harlow's ship with some of his Tarentine friends. No one was hurt, but *Pechmo* managed to steal one of Harlow's ship tenders. Harlow then sailed to Cape Cod, where he captured another Indian, and two more at the island of Martha's Vineyard. These two were *"Sachems,"* or high chiefs, *"Coneconam of Monomet"* (Cape Cod) and *"Epanow of Chapawick"* (Martha's Vineyard). He first tried to sell them as slaves in Spain, but unsuccessful there, brought them back to England and displayed them in London theaters, drawing large crowds. Then he sold them to Sir Gorges.

It was the statuesque *Epanow* who revealed to Gorges what

the English financier was craving to hear. This great Sachem knew of Norumbega and would show Gorges' men its gold-mine. It was hidden, *Epanow* told him, and was located North of his island of *Chapawick.* Gorges had his trusted Captain Holson take *Epanow* aboard his ship, *"wearing a long garment that made it difficult for the savage to walk, and might easily be laid hold of if the occasion should require."* Captain Holson also mentions that as they approached the New England coast, *"every precaution was taken to prevent Epanow's escape."* Coming to his island, *"his friends being all come in twenty canoes,"* reported Holson, *"we invited them aboard, but they did not stir."* In a great show of strength, *Epanow "knocking away two guards, leaped overboard and swam to a canoe, as the savages showered us with arrows, and we fired our muskets,"* but the clever *Epanow* made good his escape. Upon hearing the sad news when Holson returned to Plymouth, England, Gorges sighed, *"Thus, my hopes of that voyage are made void and frustrate."*

In his last ditch attempt to locate the gold rich Norumbega, Gorges sent trader Captain Thomas Dermer to meet with *Epanow* in 1619. Gorges hoped that the years that had passed since his kidnapping and escape, might have mellowed the Indian Chief, but *Epanow* was not one to forgive and forget. When Dermer and his men arrived at *Chapawick* Island, *"he was assualted by the Indians there, and all his men slain, but one that kept the boat."* Dermer managed to get back to the boat although he was, *"very sore wounded,"* and had his one remaining crewman not *"rescued him with a sword,"* he would have been killed or captured. Dermer and his man *"got away and made shift to get into Virginia, where, whether of his wounds or of a disease, he died."* Before his death, Dermer wrote to Gorges about the attack, and in the letter he mentions that *Epanow* and his warriors *"bear an inveterate malice to the English"* — and who would blame them!

It was probably Dermer's demise that decided Gorges to give up his quest for Norumbega, and the following year he concentrated his energies on shipping out some 100 religious Separatists who wanted to settle in the New World. They left Plymouth, England, and 66 days later ended up at Cape Cod, although their destination was Virginia. They decided to settle at *"Patuxet"* on the Bay side of the Cape, at a place John Smith had named, coincidentally, *"Plimouth,"* some six years before the Pilgrims arrived. This supposedly safe haven, was 28 miles from where *Epanow* lived, and only twelve miles from *"Monomet,"* which was captured Chief *Coneconam's* home town — and this only meant trouble for the residents of what is considered today, America's first home town.

The Spirit Pond Runestones, found by Walter Elliot near the Kennebec River, Maine, in 1971. The smallest stone reads, "Vinland 1010," and another contains line drawings of animals and Indians, "as seen by me, the Rune Monk." Photos by Malcolm Pearson, courtesy of Early Sites Research Society.

Old Gravestone on front lawn of a house at Cuttyhunk Island, reads: "In Memoriam to an Unknown Indian, a companion of Bartholomew Gosnold, in America's First English settlement, 1602." – Attacking Indians hacked a hole through this door with tomahawks during a raid on Deerfield, MA. This "Old Indian House Door" is now on display at Memorial Hall Museum, Deerfield. Photo courtesy of Pocumtuck Valley Memorial Association, Deerfield, MA. – An exact duplicate of Eric The Red's Castle Home now stands at Crocker Park, Marblehead, MA. – Rune markings, shown here, were discovered inside Newport's Viking Tower in 1944. Photo by Malcolm Pearson. – Ruins of Viking home at Ericsfiord, Greenland, photo courtesy of Early Sites Research Society, Rowley, MA.

III
NORUMBEGA'S NIGHTS OF TERROR

"I believe that this river is the one which several pilots and histor- ians call Norumbega, " wrote Samuel de Champlain in September of 1604, during his first of three exploratory voyages into New England. *"Most have described this river as large and spacious, with a number of islands, and this river must of necessity be Norumbega, for after it, there is no other, except the Kennebec, which is nearly the same latitude, but of no great size. "* Champlain was at Maine's Penobscot River, and at that point, hadn't explored any further South than the Maine coast. He realized that most French fishermen thought Norum- bega was in *"a more southern latitude, "* and in the Penobscot River he found *"few Indians"* and *"they came there for only a few months in the Summer. "* There was no *"great town thickly peopled with skilled and clever Indians who use cotton thread, "* as he was told, and the Indians wore furs, not gold. When he returned to Cape Breton, he reported to the royal French financiers of his expedition that, *"as to the peoples and the river of Norumbega, they are not the wonders described by some. I believe this region is as disagreeable in winter as is that of our settle- ment, in regard to which, we were greatly deceived. "*

Champlain returned to New England the following summer, cruis- ing further South than he had the year before, and on an island, which he named *"Bacchus, "* he found *"grape vines, the first we had seen on any of these coasts. "* South *"from the river called 'Saco' at a long river and another Bay, many Indians came to greet us. "* The Indians called themselves *"Almouchiquois"* and the river they called, *"Choacoet, "* but Champlain and his Canadian Indian guides had a difficult time understanding them, *"for they spoke a language different from the Etechemins"* — Maine *"canoe Indians. "* The Indians here were also different in other respects. *"These are fairly good looking, "* wrote Champlain, *"and shave off their hair fairly high up on their heads. . . They are an active people with well formed bodies, and they till and cultivate the land, a practice we have not seen previously. In place of ploughs, they use an instrument made the shape of a spade, and they keep the ground very free from weeds. These Indians remain perman- ently in this place and have large wigwams surrounded with palisades. The climate is more temperate and the place very pleasant, as attractive a spot as one can see anywhere. "* Sailing slowly South they came to *"a Cape with two or three high islands, and to the westward, a large bay, "* sounding much like Thorvald's *"pleasant land"* — this was Cape Ann, Massachusetts. Stopping to eat fruit and vegetables with the Indians, including an artichoke from their garden, he sailed on to another cape, which he called *"White Cape."* This is obviously Cape Cod, and he noted that along the way from Cape to Cape, *"there is much cleared land sown with Indian corn, and it is more populous here."*

At Cape Cod, Champlain writes that, *"we came to a sandy coast with wigwams and gardens, but we couldn't get in a river at the Indians' urgings, because the tide was out. We discovered that this was not a river but only a break in the extensive sand dunes, and the water receded and left here"* — sounding much like the landfall of Leif Ericson some 600 years before. Champlain anchored his ship and went ashore in the ship's tender to *"a bay with wigwams boardering all around."* The Indians *"were friendly, dancing and singing for us. Their fields were planted with corn five and one-half feet tall, and some less advanced which they sow later. Their wigwams are round with an opening in the middle, through which issues the smoke of their fires. They indicated little snow in the Winter, and their harbour is never froze over."* Before Champlain turned his ship around and headed back for Maine and Cape Breton, he noted in his journal that the Cape Cod Indians; *"cut off the hair on top their heads, paint their faces red, black and yellow, and have almost no beard, and pull it out as fast as it grows on their faces."* Why Champlain noticed whiskers, which the Indians plucked out, is not known, except that it was unusual to find an Indian that could grow hair on his face, unless some time in his ancestory his people had mixed with the white race. It is interesting to note that in other countries, such as England, Ireland, France and Iceland, the invading Vikings eventually mixed with the inhabitants of those countries and became part of their cultures, and there is good possibility that this is what happened to the Vikings in New England as well.

In the Autumn of 1605, hoping to explore further South, Champlain arrived back at Cape Cod. He sailed his ship around the tip and headed down the Cape's seaward or outer side, until he got to *Monomoy*, which was then connected to what is now Chatham. (Monomoy separated from the mainland in a 1958 storm, turning it into two islands nine miles long.) Here, Champlain tells us, *"the sea was breaking everywhere, and we were caught among the breakers and sand-banks. We succeeded in passing over a sandy point, but it is a very dangerous place."* It was also dangerous in other ways: *"There were six-hundred Indians at this place, who told us that at high tide we could enter their port. . . These people have olive-colored skin, are well proportioned, and go naked, but they adorn themselves with feathers, wampum beads, and other knick-knacks. . . This would be a very good site for constructing foundations of a State, except for the entrance to the harbour."*

After a few days of trading trinkets with these *"Monomoyick"* Indians, Champlain noticed *"they were taking down their wigwams and sending their wives, children and provisions into the woods. This made us suspect some evil design. Knowing that the Indians only put their plans into execution at night or at daybreak, we boarded our vessel,"* but five of his men refused to board the ship, not believing these friendly Indians would attack them. The ship's baker, who was making bread and biscuits in an Indian oven, also remained on shore. They were *"eating biscuits on shore by the fire, when the Indians shot such a salvo of arrows at them as to give them no chance of recovery. Fleeing as fast as they could towards our boat, and crying out 'Help, they are killing us,' some of them fell dead in the water, while the rest were all pierced with arrows. These Indians made a desperate row, with war-whoops which it was terrible to hear. Our musket-men then came ashore and the Indians fled."* During the fight, some musket-men were wounded, and although Champlain was *"determined to seize a few Indians of this place as punishment for the murderous assault,"* after a few days, *"the stench from wounds in our small vessel was so great that we could scarcely bear it."* They tried unsuccessfully to capture some Indians, but soon *"took a direct route back to Norumbega and Isle de Haute."* Even though France claimed New England after Champlain's first voyage here, after his Indian encounter at what he called "Misfortune Bay," France was not interested in Southern New England.

Champlain founded a new village further North, at a place called *"Quebec"* by the Indians, meaning *"where the waters narrow."* In 1609, the *Algonquin* chiefs of the Ottawa River begged him to lead them in battle against their ancient enemy the *Iroquois*. The *Iroquois* were the most feared of all New England Indians, and the fiercest of them were the *Mohawks,* who called themselves *"Ongwe-Hongwe,"* meaning, *"the men surpassing all others."* The *Algonquin* nation of *Mohigans*, who once controlled the area of *"Coos"* of the upper Connecticut River, now Vermont and New Hampshire, was infested with *Mohawks*, who had come from New York. Champlain, with two of his French lieutenants, took up the challenge, and with about seventy Indians, ascended the River Sorel in his ship. Meeting a waterfall that stopped their progress, they all took to birch-bark canoes and entered a great lake, which today bears his name — Lake Champlain, Vermont. On July 4th, they built a *"picket fort"* at Crown Point on the shore of the lake, and *"at nightfall in canoes, we advanced noiselessly and encountered a war party of Iroquois. They sent out two canoes from the Western shore to ask if the Algonquins would fight. They said that as soon as the sun should rise, they would attack us, and to this our Indians agreed."* No one slept that night, for the Indians on both sides kept shouting insults at each other across the lake, *"we and the Algonquins in canoes lashed together offshore."*

At Dawn, Champlain and his two lieutenants, dressed in light armour and carrying short muskets, went ashore with the Indians. The *Iroquois, "some 200 strong, came slowly towards us from their barricade, with a gravity and calm which I admired. Our Indians likewise advanced... I marched on until I was within some thirty yards from our enemy, and when I saw them make a move to draw their bows, I took aim with my musket and shot straight at one of their three chiefs, and with this shot, two fell to the ground and one other was wounded. Meanwhile, the arrows flew thick on both sides. The Iroquois were much astounded, and seeing their chief dead, they lost courage and took to flight into the forest, wither I pursued and laid low still more of them. Our Indians also killed several and took twelve prisoners."*

That night, camped at Otter Creek, *"the Algonquins took one of the prisoners to torture, and they ordered him to sing. He did so, but it was a very sad song to hear. Each Indian took and burned this poor wretch a little at a time. Then they tore out his nails and applied fire to the ends of his fingers. Afterwards they scalped him and caused a certain kind of gum to drop very hot upon the crown of his head. Then they pierced his arms near the wrists and with sticks pulled and tore out his sinews by main force, and when they saw that they could not get them out, they cut them off. This poor wretch uttered strange cries, and I felt pity at seeing him treated this way. Still, he bore it so firmly that sometimes one would have said he felt scarcely any pain. I went away, angry at seeing them practice so much cruelty. When they saw I was not pleased, they called me back and told me to give him a shot with my musket, which I did..."* Thus, Champlain was the first to witness and record one of the Indians most popular spectator sports. It was a scene that was to be repeated many times before the New England colonies were safely settled. This first French-*Algonquin* battle against the *Iroquois*, prompted the *Iroquois* to join the English, and was the stimulous for a war between these allied groups that lasted until 1763.

"We find the Indians of New England very kind," wrote John Smith, who sailed with a fleet of vessels from Penobscot, Maine to Cape Cod, surveying and mapping the coast in the summer of 1614. *"But,"* he adds, in his book, *"A Description of New England,"* the Indians here, *"in their fury are no less valiant. Upon a quarrel we had with one of*

them, he along with three others, crossed the harbor of Quonahassit (Cohasset, South of Boston) *to certain rocks whereby we had to pass, and there let fly their arrows, until we were out of range."* A few days later, some forty Indians attacked Smith and his crew near this same place, and one Indian was killed. Yet, writes Smith, *"within one hour the Indians made friends again."* He called the Boston area, *"the paradise of all these parts, with a good harbor and a large population of friendly Indians, already surviving on cultivated fields."* Yet, about this same time, Cotton Mather writes that *"a Monsieur Finch, trading with the Massachusetts Indians at Boston, was butchered with his men, and their ship set on fire."* At Peddock's Island, *"those bloody savages,"* writes Mather, *"coming on board without any arms, but with knives concealed under flaps."* Thomas Morton, in his book, *"New Canaan,"* published in 1637, adds to Mather's story, that five Frenchmen aboard Finch's ship, were taken captive. *"They were made to fetch the Indians food and water,"* writes Morton, *"for as long as they lived. One of the five having outlived the rest, he rebuked them for their bloody deed, saying that God would be angry with them for it, and that He would in his displeasure destroy them. But the savages, it seems, boasting of their strength, replied and said that they were too many, and that God could not kill them."*

Shortly after Smith completed his three months of exploring and mapping the New England coast to Cape Cod, he sailed his ship to Virginia, but one of his vessels, with Captain Thomas Hunt in command, remained at *Patuxet* (Plymouth). Hunt then proceeded to kidnap 27 Indians, twenty at *Patuxet* and seven more at *Nauset* on the Cape. He shipped then to England, where most were sold as slaves. Hearing of Hunt's crime, Smith was furious, but there was little he could do about it. At about the same time in 1614, a Dutchman named Adrian Block was exploring and trading with the Indians for furs in Connecticut. He discovered the little island off Rhode Island, which is named for him, and sailed the Connecticut River where, near Hartford, he encountered a large Indian village and fort. Estimates at the time were that some 10,000 Indians lived in this part of Connecticut. The warning to the Boston Indians by the last remaining Frenchman of Finch's crew, however, proved prophetic; — within two years of Block's visit, there were but 2,000 Indians along the Connecticut coast. The coasts of Maine, Massachusetts, Rhode Island, and New Hampshire were also devastated with a plague that killed some 80% of the Indian population. *"God fell heavily upon them,"* wrote Thomas Morton, *"with such a mortal stroke that they died in heaps. In places where many inhabited, there hath been but one left alive."* Smith viewed this plague on the New

England Indians not as a curse from the heavens on them, but as a blessing to the English. *"It seems,"* he said, *"as if God hath provided this New England country for our nation, destroying the natives by the plague."*

To add to the tragedy of the *Massachusetts* Indians, another killer invaded just as the plague was subsiding. The *Tarentines* of Maine swooped down on the weakened tribes of Massachusetts to steal their corn and to beat them into everlasting submission. Thousands of them came in bark canoes, first hitting the *Agawams* from Newburyport to Beverly, including the Indians of Cape Ann, and then the main fortress of the *Massachusetts* nation at what is now Castle Hill in Salem, Massachusetts. The Sachem of Massachusetts, *Nanepshemet,* held out at Castle Hill for weeks, but then he and his warriors were pushed all the way back to Boston's Mystic River. The war lasted for almost three years, and in 1618, *Nanepahemet* was slain in a battle at Saugus. The *Massachusetts nation* was defeated, its many tribes and subtribes greatly reduced in number. Even the *Pokanokets,* who lived on the Rhode Island border, were attacked by the *Tarentines*, although they were not part of the *Massachusetts nation.* Their chief, *Massasoit,* led his warriors to victory, but not without heavy losses. The *Tarentines* paddled back to Maine to lick their wounds, but promised to return. With the once great *Massachusetts nation* devastated, *Massasoit's Pokanokets*, also known as *Wampanoags,* were now *"of more strength than all the savages from thence to Penobscot."* Living across the bay from *Massasoit,* however, were the *Narragansetts* of Rhode Island, who remained powerful and were his enemy.

After the killing, kidnapping and looting by the *Tarentines,* the remnants of the *Massachusetts* nation, from Quincy to Salem, was led by the three sons of *Nanepshemet,* and the Sachem's wife. They divided the land into four tribal territories. The youngest son, *Winepoykin,* who was just a teenager, became chief of the *Nahumkeikes* of Salem and Marblehead, with his mother in command as *"squaw sachem"* from Lynn to Concord, of the *Saugus* tribal lands. *Winepoykin* in battle had his nose sliced off by a *Tarentine,* and when the English settled at *Nahumkeik,* they nick-named him, *"No-Nose George."* He made his home on a small penninsula between what is now the North, Bass and Danvers Rivers, with some 600 members of his subtribe. The Indian name for the combined Danvers and Bass Rivers that flowed beside their village, was *"Nahumkeika,"* sounding much like the great river *Norumbega,* that all the great European explorers had been searching for. The *Nahumkeika River* separates Salem and Beverly,

Massachusetts, and flows into Beverly Harbor, after joining forces with the North River. Beyond Beverly Harbor, where the waters of the South and Forest Rivers flow into Salem Harbor, they all meet at a Y and flow beyond the many islands to the open sea, only six miles Southwest of Cape Ann. It was the one great harbor mouth that all the early explorers had missed, either sailing directly from Cape Ann to Cape Cod, or stopping off at what is now Boston. Could it be that *Nahumkega*, was really *"the golden city of Norumbega,"* originally spelled and pronounced *"Nahumbeak"* in early 16th century Europe, which today is the city of Salem, Massachusetts?

"Settling at Plimouth was a fatal blunder," Miles Standish, military leader of the Plymouth Plantation, told Governor Bradford in July of 1621. He had been exploring up to sixty miles north of their settlement and found *"Nahumkeike to have better lands and forests for farming and hunting, and its magnificent harbor would provide better fishing."* Bradford decided that they should stay where they were. Standish was disappointed. He sailed to Cape Ann, where a small group of fishermen from Dorchester, England were building a house and a salt works to preserve codfish. They had been catching cod there since 1616. They usually sailed back to England in the Autumn with their catch, but in the winter of 1622, they decided to live the winter at Cape Ann. *"These land men were ill commanded and commenced falling into many disorders,"* the Pilgrims of Plymouth were informed, and Roger Conant, *"a sober and prudent gentleman,"* who lived at *Nantasket*, was asked to move to Cape Ann and take command of the fishermen. The fishing colony failed, and Miles Standish tried unsuccessfully to save it. Conant, like most early settlers, didn't get along with the little quick-tempered Miles Standish, and Conant moved out of Cape Ann, to Naumkeag, *"a fruitful neck of land,"* with 25 of his followers, women and children included. By the winter of 1626, their new *"whiteman's wigwams"* were built on the banks of the North River where it meets the *Nahumkeika* River, facing No-Nose George's Indian village. Conant found *Winepoykin* and his tribe to be friendly and helpful. and not warlike at all.

Two years later, September 6, 1628, fifty more settlers from England arrived at Naumkeag, with the newly appointed Governor of the Mass Bay Company, John Endicott. His orders from England were to establish America's first commercial outpost, and in the process, New England's first Town. Conant and Endicott immediately disagreed over land grants, and the laws these new Puritans were bound to follow. Conant wanted to grow tobacco at Naumkeag like the Indians did, but Endicott considered it an *"unholy weed."* The two men argued and discussed for almost an entire day, and came to a somewhat amiable agreement, Conant eventually moving across the bay to the banks of the Bass River, and Endicott changing the name of Naumkeag to Salem — the Hebrew word for *"peace."* All this being done without the advice or consent of *Winepoykin.*

Meanwhile, the Pilgrims were having a few problems with their Indian neighbors. Their first encounter with *"the savages,"* was in November of 1620, before they decided to settle at Plymouth. The Mayflower was anchored off Provincetown, when Standish, with 16 of his musketeers, saw *"five or six savages run into the woods from the beach."* A dog was with them, *"and it followed when they whistled for it."* The Pilgrims chased the Indians for an entire day, fearing that they would be ambushed, but never catching sight of them again. It was then that they got lost in what is now Truro, and robbed Indian mounds of corn, a burial site of trinkets, and took objects found in an abandoned wigwam. *"We also digged a place a little further off and found a bottle of oil."* Four weeks later at Wellfleet, *"All of a sudden we heard a great and strange cry,"* reports Pilgrim Edward Winslow, who later became a Governor of Plymouth; *"One of our Company came running and said, 'Indians!,' and withal, their arrows came flying amongst us. The cry of our enemies was dreadful, especially when our men ran to recover their arms, which they lay on the shore at a little distance. In the meantime, Captain Miles Standish made a shot, and after him, another. Only four of us had their arms ready, and stood before the open side of the barricade, which was first assaulted. There was a lusty Indian who stood behind a tree within half a musket-shot of us, and there let his arrows fly at us. He stood three shots of a musket. At length one took, and he gave an extraordinary cry, and away they all went. None of their arrows hit us, though many came close by on every side of us . . . "* Winslow adds that, *"some of the arrows were tipped with brass points."*

The next sound the Pilgrims heard from an Indian was four months later, after half of them had died over the winter at Plymouth — they were the words, *"Welcome Englishmen."* *"We were interrupted and alarmed,"* says Winslow, *"by a savage, stark naked, only for leather about his waist, who very boldly came alone, and along the houses straight to the rendeyvous, where we intercepted him... He saluted us in English and bade us welcome, for he had learned some broken English among those that came to fish at Monchiggon,"* (Monhegan Island, Maine). Their visitor was *Samoset,* a Sagamore of Maine, who had been wandering New England for some eight months, and as he said, had *"discovered the whole country"* ... *"He carried a bow and two arrows,"* wrote Winslow, *"and was a tall straight man. The hair of his head black, and long behind, only short before, none on his face at all. He asked for some beer, but we gave him strong water, .. He told us that the place where we now lived is called Patuxet, and that about four years ago, all the inhabitants died of an extraordinary plague. All the afternoon we spent in communications with him. We would gladly have been rid of him at night, but he was not willing to go. We lodged him that night at Stephen Hopkin's house, and watched him."*

This *"foreign"* Maine Indian, was a blessing in disguise to the Pilgrims in many ways, and although the Pilgrims wondered why the neighboring Indians hadn't shown themselves for some four months, it wasn't until years later that Governor Bradford found out the reason. A few weeks after the Pilgrims arrived, the *"Powachees,"* known to the whites as witch-doctors and medicinemen, had met, *"in a dark and dismale swamp together for three days,"* to plan death and destruction of the white visitors.

It was *Samoset* who, after leaving the plantation, sent word to *Sachem Massasoit,* to tell him that the Pilgrims came in peace. *Samoset* returned to Plymouth with a local Indian named *Squanto,* who spoke English well, for he had been one of the *Patuxets* captured by Captain Hunt and brought to England in 1614, and had been returned home by Captain Dermer only two years before, thus missing the plague, which wiped out his people. Also with *Samoset* on his second visit to Plymouth were five other Indians. It was *Squanto,* with another called *Hobbomuk,* who finally taught the Pilgrims how to trap, tap maple syrup from the trees, plant Indian corn, and fertilize their ground with fish and lobster. Bradford wrote of the Indians *Samoset* brought with him; *"they are the complexion of our English gypsies, dressed in skins and wearing long stockings of leather to their groins, altogether like Irish trousers. Some trussed up their hair before with a feather broadwise like a fan, another had a fox-tail hanging out and some had black painted faces."* They sang and danced for the Pilgrims, and five days later, the great tall *Sachem, Massasoit,* with his colorful 60-man entourage arrived. What surprised the Pilgrims most about *Massasoit* was that he had a thick beard. Historians have speculated that his father might have been a white man, but it could be that his ancestors were Vikings. A cordial peace treaty was made between Pilgrims and *Wampanaogs*, and *Massasoit* returned to his home village at *Sowans* forty miles away on Narragansett Bay — now Warren, Rhode Island.

The *Narragansett* Indians, however, *"who had not been touched by the wasting plague,"* sent a messenger to the Pilgrims shortly after *Massasoit's* departure. The messenger handed the Pilgrim fathers *"a bundle of arrows tied about with a great snakeskin,"* which *Squanto* told them was a challenge of war. The messenger was informed that the Pilgrims prefered peace and *"had done them no wrong, but neither did we fear the Narragansetts."* The Pilgrims then returned the snakeskin package with musketballs and gun powder tucked into it — and they heard no more from the *Narragansetts,* but the message prompted Miles Standish to build a surrounding fence and a timber fort at the plantation. On September 13, 100 Indians from various neighboring tribes came to Plymouth, and nine Sachems signed a treaty of submission to the King of England. Among them was *Coneconam* of Monomet, who Sir Gorges held captive after he was kidnapped from New England in 1611, and Sir Gorges' famed escapee, *Epanow* of Martha's Vineyard. They had come at *Massasoit's* prompting. The great Sachem of the *Wampanoags* feared that his federation of tribes that extended to Cape Cod, Plymouth and the islands, would be attacked by the *Narragansetts,* if they did not join the white men as allies. The *Narragansetts* did, however, attack one of *Massasoit's* islands the following year.

While the Pilgrims satisfied themselves signing peace treaties with the Indians, Sir Gorges, who held royal title from King James I to *"all lands from the Merrimack to the Kennebec Rivers thence to the Great Lakes,"* was sending over fishermen, traders, and farmers to settle his land. Fishing colonies were started at the Isles of Shoals and at Strawberry Bank in *Piscataqua* (Portsmouth, New Hampshire) in 1623, and extended to Dover, Exeter, and Hampton, New Hampshire within fifteen years. The real owner of these lands, however, was the Great Sachem *Pasaconnaway* of the *Pennacook* tribe. Yet he, like most Indians, had little concept of land ownership. These were fishing and hunting territories, and when the English eventually paid a few dollars and trinkets for them, most Indians didn't realize that these lands would be lost to them forever. As all his land along the Merrimack River was taken over by English settlers, *Pasaconnaway* gathered his tribe at *Pawtucket Falls,* now Lowell, Massachusetts, and said to them that, *"when the English came I made war with them. They seized the lands and they fought me with fire and thunder. I tried sorcery against them but they still increased, and prevailed over me and mine. Now I am powerless against these pale faces, and I must bend before the storm..."*

The only tribe the *Tarrentines* of Maine feared, was their New Hampshire neighbors, the *Pennacooks,* but only because of *Passaconnaway.* He was not just a strong Sachem, but the most powerful *"Powahee,"* or as the English called him, *"prophet and magic maker,"* in New England. Among other things, he could *"make fire in snow,"* and *"cuddle venomous snakes,"* and most important to the Indians, he could accurately predict future events. When a comet appeared in the New England sky in 1616, he predicted it as an evil omen of the coming plague that would destroy two-thirds of the coastal Indians. When musketmen from Boston came to arrest him in 1642 for stirring up trouble, he stopped them with a violent storm, which lasted just long enough for him to escape, although his son *Wonolancet* was captured and brought to Boston for questioning. *"A Powahee,"* wrote Thomas Lechford that same year, *"labors himself into incantations of extreme sweating and weariness, even to ecstasy. He usually has many wives, and Indians say that Powahees commit much filthyness among themselves."* In all tribes, the *Powahee* was almost as powerful as the Sachem, and more so than the Sagamore, who was prince or councilor of the tribe. *Passaconnaway* was all these powers in one, however, after listening to John Elliot, New England's *"white Indian Apostle,"* he converted to Christianity, and began listening to a higher power. *"Peace with the white man is the command of the Great Spirit,"* he told Elliot, *"and the final wish of Passaconnaway."*

Living along the coastal lands between *Passaconnaway's Penna-cooks* and *Winepoykin's Nahumkeikes,* were the *Agawams* — *"fish curing people."* Their Sachem was *Masconomet,* who ruled all of Cape Ann, from Beverly to Newbury, with his main village in what is today, Hamilton, Massachusetts. He, like *Winepoykin* (No-Nose George) was very fearful of the Maine *Tarentines,* and like *Massasoit,* accepted the new white settlers as protectors and buffers against age old Indian enemies. When the new Governor, John Winthrop, of the Mass Bay Company, arrived on the Arbella on June 12, 1630, it was *Masconomet,* not *No-Nose George* who greeted him at Manchester and made him welcome, assuring Winthrop that *"there will be no trouble between your people and my people."* Winthrop had come to settle at Salem, replacing Endicott as Governor. Arriving at Salem 17 days later was the ship Talbot and four other vessels, with almost 1,000 new settlers. Aboard the Talbot was Governor Winthrop's son Henry, whose first desire in the New World was to see *No-Nose George* and his tribe of *Nahumkeikes.* While crossing the North River in a canoe, it capsized and Henry drowned. A few days later, the Governor left Salem to relocate the seat of government at Charlestown, and then across the river to *Shawmut,* known today as Boston — Thus, Salem - possibly the mysterious golden city of Norumbega- missed becoming the capital of Massachusetts and the famed *"Hub of the New World."*

The following year, on August 8th, the *Tarentines* struck again, about 100 of them in canoes, invading the *Agawams*. As was their custom, they came at night, and as Winthrop tells us, *"assaulted the wigwam of the Sagamore of Agawam by the Merrimack, and slew seven men, and wounded John Sagamore, and James, and some others, whereof some died after, and rifled a wigwam where Mr. Cradock's men kept to catch sturgeon."* They also captured a squaw, who they may have realized was Sachem *Passaconnway's* daughter. She was the wife of *Montowawpate*, also known as *Sagamore James of Saugus*, who was wounded in the battle with the *Tarentines*. *Masconomet* took credit for killing many of the *Tarentines* and making them retreat back to their canoes. Winthrop writes in his Journal that nine days later, *"Mr. Shurd of Pemaquid sent home James Sagamore's wife, who had been taken away at the surprise at Agawam."* Actually the *Tarentines* had held her for ransom, and *Masconomet* paid wampum, kettles and other trinkets to get her back for *Montowawpate*. *Passaconnaway*, it seems, did not involve himself in the ransom demand, nor did *No-Nose George*, who was *Sagamore James'* brother. As Lechford explains, *"Indian women do most of the labor while the men are idle, and squaws are held in great slavery. The Indians here say that English men are much fools for spoiling good working creatures, meaning women."*

The *Tarentines* also attempted to invade Ispwich, which then had only thirty white settlers. An *Agawam* Indian named *Robin* saw *"forty canoes filled with armed Tarentines coming up the Ipswich River and warned John Perkins."* Many of the men were away, but Perkins had those who were at home fire their muskets and beat drums, *"and the noise frightened the Indians off."* It was after this episode that *Masconomet* came to the settlers of Ipswich and asked to remain with them under their protection. The Puritan ministers decided that this was an excellent opportunity to convert *Masconomet* to Christianity, hoping that all the *Agawams* would then follow his example. They told the Sachem that they would protect him forever from the *Tarentines* if he, forever, would follow their religion. *"Will you refrain from working on a Sunday?"* was one of the questions put to him before he became a Christian. *"Yes,"* he replied. *"It is easy for me and my warriors, for we have not much to do any day, and we can rest on that day."* In 1638, John Winthrop bought *Agawam* (Ipswich and Essex) from *Masconomet* for twenty pounds, and later, the settlers paid fourteen pounds for Beverly and all of Cape Ann. A year after *Masconomet* died, in 1659, English settlers dug up his body at Sagamore Hill in Hamilton and carried his skull on a pole through Ipswich just for sport.

No-Nose George was as peace-loving as *Masconomet*, yet Englishman John Josselyn who visited *Agawam* and *Naumkeag* in 1638 said that, *"they are cannibals, eaters of human flesh,"* and that a *Tarentine* captured by them, *"was tortured unmercifully. Then they cut out his heart, and it was bitten into by every old squaw."* John Woodbury, who lived at *Naumkeag* in 1627, thought *No-Nose George's* Indians were lazy and called them *"silly savages,"* seemingly *"frightened of everything."* *"They speak in grunts and groans,"* wrote Woodbury, *"and while the squaws do all the work, the men seem more interested in lazing about, fishing now and then and drinking uncuppy"* — liquor. Said Thomas Lechford, *"Seldom are they abroad in the extremity of Winter, but keep to their wigwams, till necessity drives them forth. They are naturally proud and idle, and given much to singing, dancing and plays."* The *Naumkeags* were such a fearful people that they would not venture out of their wigwams at night, and if they happened to be away from their village, they would walk into any wigwam or settlers' home when the sun went down. The situation at Salem became so outrageous that the Town fathers passed an ordinance warning every *Naumkeag* Indian that *"he must knock on a house door and be invited in, before entering and making himself comfortable by the fireside."* The penalty for disobeying the Salem ordinance was a fine of one basket of corn. The *Naumkeags,* like most of the once powerful *Massachusetts* nation, *"were like children"* and many white settlers treated them as such. Some treated them with scorn and cruelty. Their fear of the dark apparently resulted from their nightmarish defeat by the *Tarentines,* who, as Governor Bradford remarked, *"came to reap what they have not sown, and brought great fear to the Massachusetts nation."*

When the old prophet *Passaconnaway* died in 1666, at age 120, John Elliot reported that his last words to the *Pennacooks* were, *"take heed how much you quarel with the English, for though you may do them much mischief, assuredly you will be destroyed and rooted off the earth if you do."* This was the warning of the greatest *Powahee,* sounding the death knell for his race. He was a greater prophet than he realized — for, ten years from his death, his people were *"rooted off the earth,"* even the *"fearful, lazy, peaceful"* ones.

IV
THE MISCHIEF OF METACOMET

Massasoit, Sachem of the Wampanoags, told the Pilgrims many times that he wanted nothing to do with Christian religions. Yet, one day he walked the forty miles from his village to Plymouth with his two oldest sons so that the Pilgrims could personally give his sons Christian names. This surprising request pleased the people of Plymouth Plantation and strengthened their trust in *Massasoit.* The Christian name given to the eldest son *Wamsutta,* was *"Alexander,"* and to *Metacomet,* the second oldest, the Pilgrims offered the name *"Philip"* — after Alexander the Great and his father Philip. Following this gesture, it seemed that only *Squanto,* who lived at Plymouth, continued to show a mistrust of *Massasoit.* He told the Pilgrims that the *Wampanoags* with other tribes from the *Massachusetts* and *Narragansett* nations planned to attack Plymouth, but when confronted, *Massasoit* called *Squanto* a liar. He asked the Pilgrims to turn *Squanto* over to him so he could chop off his head. The Pilgrims of course refused, for even if *Squanto* stretched the truth now and then, he was invaluable to them.

In the autumn of 1622, *Squanto* was asked to lead a sailing expedition to Cape Cod and Rhode Island to barter for food with the Indians there, so that the Plymouth Pilgrims and especially the new settlers at *Wessagusett,* (Weymouth) could get through the coming winter. The Pilgrims were not too pleased with the 60 men who had started a tradingpost at *Wessagusett,* for they were *"wild men,"* Governor Bradford said, *"gotten from the taverns of London,"* and in the year since they had arrived, were not able to provide food enough for themselves. The only reason Bradford agreed to a joint food procuring expedition was that the *Wessagusett* men volunteered their sturdy ship, the Swan. The joint venture was successful, the Cape Cod Indians more than willing to give up corn and beans for trinkets, but the journey cost the Pilgrims their dearest possession — *Squanto.* He died suddenly and without apparent cause, while aboard the Swan.

The following March, word came to Plymouth that *Massasoit* was dying. Pilgrims Winslow and Hampden were sent with medicine and herb broth to *Sowans* in an attempt to save him. They found the great *Sachem* had lost his eyesight and was all but choking on his own flem. The homemade broth worked, and within a day *Massasoit* regained his sight and his spunkiness. *"I will never forget this kindness,"* he told Winslow. Then he proceeded to tell the Pilgrims who had saved his life, that as *Squanto* had warned, certain Indians were going to attack and kill the white men, but not at Plymouth— at *Wessagusett*. The trading-post men were starving once again, and some had sold themselves as slaves to tribes of the *Massachusetts* nation for food to survive. One of the *Wessagusett* men had been caught raiding an Indian corn mound, and the Indian *Sachem Chikataubut* demanded he be hanged. The settlers agreed to hang the young thief, but before the *Sachem* and his tribe gathered to witness the hanging, the men at the tradingpost dressed an old ill man in the young victim's clothes. They told the old man that they just wanted to fool the Indians, but proceeded to hang him. This delighted the Indians, who didn't realize that an old weak man had died in the place of the young strong man who had stolen their corn.

Massasoit named three Indians who were scheming to wipe out the entire tradingpost. They were *Sachem Wituwamat* of a *Massachusetts* subtribe, *Pecksuot*, a hater of white men, who blamed the English for the plague, and *Coneconam* of *Manomet*, Sir Gorges' old house guest. Winslow rushed back to Plymouth to tell Miles Standish of the plot on *Wessagusett*.

When Standish arrived with eight armed Pilgrims at the trading-post, only twenty of the traders were there, living on acorns. *Wituwamat* and *Pecksuot*, with *Wituwamat's* 15-year-old brother soon showed up and started calling Standish unflattering names. The little captain held his temper and invited the three Indians into the tradingpost to eat pork with him. The surley Indians, who loved pork, gladly joined him at the dinner table. Once inside the tradingpost, Standish jumped *Peksuot* and wrestled him to the floor, stabbing him with his own knife. Two of Standish's men took on *Wituwamat*, who had earlier called them *"cowards,"* and after a long struggle, killed him. Says Winslow, who was there to watch this battle, *"It is incredible how many wounds these two Panieses* (men of valor) *received before they died, not making any fearful noise, but clutching their weapons, and strong to the last."* Standish then dragged the bodies outside and sent messengers to invite all neighboring Indians to the tradingpost. Once they had arrived, Standish cut off *Wituwamat's* head and mounted it on a pole. Then, he brought forth the headless *Sachem's* 15-year-old brother and hanged him from the nearest tree. Hearing the news, *Sachem Chickataubut* killed his three white slaves from *Wessagusett*, and then took his tribe into the woods to hide. *Coneconam* also hid in a swamp fearing the wrath of Standish, and there died of starvation. As Standish realized, because of his bold, if not sneaky attack, he would now get respect from the local Indians. *Witawamat's* head was displayed outside the Plymouth fort for many years as a reminder to visiting Indians.

New white settlements began cropping up throughout New England, mostly offshoots of Plymouth Plantation and the Mass Bay Colonies. A Welch minister, Roger Williams, who was kicked out of Plymouth and Salem for preaching Indian rights and separation of church and state, wandered through the wilderness, *"on foot in the dead of winter,"* arriving at *Sowams*. *Massasoit* not only gave him asylum, but gave him land in Rhode Island, where Willams started a settlement of religious dissidents. At Tiverton and Providence, he not only welcomed men and women of all religions, but made peace with the neighboring *Narragansetts*. At about the same time, new settlements were sprouting up at Hartford, Windham, Saybrook, and New Haven, Connecticut, at the displeasure of the *Pequot* Indians, who thought the whites were infringing on their land — which they were. The first incident that sparked a war between Pilgrim — Puritan forces and *Pequots,* had nothing to do with the *Pequot* Indians at all.

John Oldham, who, like Roger Williams, had been kicked out of Plymouth because of disagreements with Miles Standish, settled at *Nantasket* and often sailed to Rhode Island and Connecticut to trade with the Indians. At *Munisses,* (Block Island) he was attacked by a band of renegade Indians and was killed. His two young sons were taken captive. The culprits were *Narragansett* Indians, but their *Sachem Canonicus* told the Governor that they were just a few rebellious tribe members, who *Canonicus* would punish. The *Sachem* sent his nephew, *Miantonomo,* with many braves and some white settlers to Block Island, where they rescued Oldham's two sons, slaughtered many Indians, and torched their village. They never did, however, find and punish the renegades who murdered John Oldham. On the way home to their settlements after the revenge at *Munisses,* some of the white soldiers trampled gardens belonging to the *Pequots,* and this infuriated *Sassacus* their *Sachem.*

The *Pequots* retaliated, and in a surprise attack, raided the white settlements at Saybrook and Wethersfield, Connecticut. At Wethersfield they, *"roasted alive the inhabitants,"* by setting fire to the houses and barns, and they captured and carried off two young women. One of them who was kept as a slave in a *Pequot* viliage for three months, later reported, *"I have been in the midst of those roaring lions and savage bears day and night, and sleeping all sorts together, yet not one of them ever offered the least abuse of unchastity to me."*

Connecticut and Massachusetts declared war on the *Pequots.* The *Mohigan* Indians, under *Sachem Uncas,* joined the Connecticut troops, and the *Narragansetts,* who hated the *Pequots* as much as they did the *Wampanoags,* sided with Captain John Underhill and his Massachusetts men. A combined force of 100 whites and 700 allied Indians, in March of 1637, marched to the *Pequot* fort and village at Mystic, Connecticut. When they attacked at dawn, the *Pequots* inside the palisades were asleep. First, Underhill had firebrands thrown over the walls to set some 80 wigwams on fire, and as *Pequot* men, women, and children ran from the flames, they were shot. It was a slaughter, with some 700 *Pequots* either burning to death, or being killed with musketballs and arrows. Only two white men were killed, and twenty-two were wounded. The few *Pequot* warriors who were captured were brought to Long Island Sound, put aboard Captain Gallop's ship, and thrown overboard to drown. The *Pequot* women and children who survived were brought to Boston where they were sold as slaves. Some 200 other *Pequot* Indians surrendered at their village in New London, and some 80 remnants of the nation were killed or captured in a swamp, three months later.

Captives were divided as prisoners-of-war between the *Mohigans,* the *Narragansetts,* and their cousins, the *Niantics.* Captain Underhill, however, was disappointed with the *Narragansetts,* for unlike the *Mohigans,* they didn't participate in the massacre at Mystic, and only involved themselves in taking *Pequot* captives. Their *"Paniese," Miantonomo,* was also disappointed and disgusted, for *Uncas* and his *Mohigans* received more spoils of war than did his *Narragansetts.* This sparked a second Indian war four years later. What *Miantonomo* failed to see, or apparently didn't much care about at the time, was that the *Pequots,* a name that meant *"destroyers,"* had been completely destroyed— and his tribe would share their same fate, once he declared war on the whites and the *Mohigans.*

Uncas told the white settlers that the *Narragansetts* planned to attack settlements in Massachusetts, and *Miantonomo* was called to court in Boston, to face charges of conspiracy. This infuriated the *Narragansetts,* and after leaving the Boston court, *Miantonomo* waylaid one of the *Mohigan* accusers and chopped off his head, then he and his braves attacked *Uncas.* During the battle, *Uncas* and his warriors captured *Miantonomo* and then easily defeated the *Narragansett* warparty. *Uncas* asked permission from the court at Hartford, Connecticut to dispose of *Miantonomo.* Given permission to do so, he personally chopped off *Miantonomo's* head. *Canonicus, Sachem* of the *Narragansetts,* warned, *"I will always be at war with the Mohigans, and I will kill Engilish cattle and heap them as high as their dwellings, and no Englishman shall stir from his door to piss, but I will kill him."*

A few years later, at age 81, *Massasoit,* the *Great Sachem* of the *Wampanoags* died, and his son *Wamsutta,* alias Alexander, became

Sachem. Only a few months went by when the Pilgrim Fathers got word from some *"praying Indians,"* who had converted to Christianity and taken up white ways, that *Wamsutta* had made an alliance with his old enemy *Canonicus.* This frightened the Pilgrims and they called for *Wamsutta* to come to Plymouth to explain these accusations. *Wamsutta* refused to come to Plymouth to face unfounded charges. Major Edward Winslow with ten men was sent to fetch *Wamsutta* and bring him to Plymouth. Winslow burst into his hunting lodge, where he sat with eight of his men, and put a gun to his head, demanding that he come to Plymouth under guard. Winslow first brought him to his own house in Duxbury, where *Wamsutta* came down with a fever. He then pleaded with Winslow that he be allowed to go back to his village and return when he was feeling better. Winslow reluctantly agreed, but on his way back to *Sowans, Wamsutta* died. The *Wampanoags* were convinced that Winslow had poisoned their chief.

Metacomet, Massasoit's second son, was immediately crowned *Sachem of the Wampanoags* and was called *"King Philip"* by the English settlers. Although he often dressed in fancy white man's clothes, and feigned peace treaties with the settlers, he announced to his warriors soon after his inauguration feast that his intention was *"to make war, and drive the settlers back to England."* He, however, had only about 1,000 *Wampanoag* warriors, and he realized he would need alliances with many other Indian tribes to defeat the whites, who now numbered some 33,000 in New England. His hope was to bring in his old arch-enemy *Canonicus* with some 4,000 ready, willing and able *Narragansett* braves to join his fight, but *Canonicus,* it seems, was hedging. Many of the *"Nipmets,"* also called *"Nipmucks,"* who lived along the inland lakes of Massachusetts and Connecticut, where frontier settlements were cropping up, agreed to join *Metacomet* in an all out war. Apparently the Indian King felt he could gather many more tribes by the spring of 1676, for that was the time he set for his rising of red-man against white-man.

It was a *praying Indian, John Sausaman,* once an aide to *Metacomet,* who upset the King's plan. He went to the new Governor of Plymouth, Edward Winslow, and informed him of the Indian plot. *Metacomet* was summoned by Winslow to come to Plymouth on charges of conspiracy, but unlike his brother before him, he showed up, and swore he was innocent of the charges. Then, in January, *John Sausaman* was found murdered, his head crushed and his neck broken, on the ice of a pond in Middleborough. Another *praying Indian* had witnessed the murder from nearby woods, and accused three of *Metacomet's* most trusted warriors of the crime. The three *Wampanoag* warriors were brought to trial at Plymouth, found guilty by a jury, and were executed — two were hanged and one was shot. No sooner had the verdict been carried out than *Wampanoag* renegades attacked the settlement at Swansea near the Rhode Island border, and six farmers were killed — the war was on, sooner than even *Metacomet* expected. A combined force of 400 men and boys ages 16 to 60 from Plymouth and Boston, were hurredly assembled and marched to Swansea, and from there to *"Mountaup,"* called Mount Hope by the settlers, where *Metacomet* made his home. Instead of finding *Metacomet* and his warriors, who they had come to battle, they found empty wigwams, and the severed heads of the six farmers of Swansea, mounted on long poles.

The *Wampanoag* warriors, with their families, had crossed the waters and joined the *Pocassets,* under the *"Squaw Sachem Weetamo,"* who happened to be *"Metacomet's* sister-in-law. *Metacomet's* braves now numbered about 1,400. They headed north to join with the *Nipmets,* but along the way, raided the settlements of Taunton, Middleborough, Mendon, Dartmouth, Westport and Rehoboth. *"The enemy first began their hostilities with plundering and destroying cattle,"* writes Captain Benjamin Church, who with his men was trying to catch up with the warring Indians. *"They thirsted for English blood, and soon killed ten men at Matapoiset; Upon where, ladies they excersized more than brutish barbarities; beheading, dismembering and mangling them, and exposing them in the most inhuman manner."* At Dartmouth, he says, *"they did burn with fire and barbarously murdered both men and women, stripping the slain and leaving them in an open field."* Finding no hostile Indians at *Mount Hope, Sowans,* or *Keekamuit* (Warren, Rhode Island), Major Thomas Savage, commander of the Pilgrim-Puritan army, went to visit *Canonicus* and the *Narragansetts,* to have them sign a peace-treaty *"thus avoiding them joining Philip."*

Meanwhile, Governor John Leverett on Boston called for volunteers to fight the Indians. His brother-in-law, Captain Sam Mosley, a privateersman, was first to step forward. He hated all Indians, and within three hours he had collected 110 men, many of them sailors, and ten of them were Dutch pirates. They scrounged up muskets, swords and ten-foot pikes, plus a few dogs to frighten the Indians, and marched off to battle. Also, fifty *Mohigans,* under *Sachem Oneko,* son of *Uncas,* showed up in Boston from Connecticut, ready to fight the *Wampanoags.* They all met Commander Daniel Henchmen's militia at Rehoboth and chased after *Metacomet's* army of men, women and children, who were heading into *Nipmet* territory in Western Massachusetts. Twice, the militia and *Mohigans* caught up with the rear-guard of the *Wampan-oags*, and there were brief skirmishes, with a few on each side being killed or wounded. One Indian killed was *Sunconewhew*, brother of *Metacomet*, and youngest son of *Massasoit*. The reason why the militia and *Mohigans* never caught up with the main body of the enemy, is that the *Mohigans* would stop when an enemy was killed or wounded to plunder the belongings he carried with him and to scalp him. Four of these scalps were sent back to Governor Leverett as a prize of battle, and it is reported that he proudly displayed them to the people of Boston.

Governor Leverett sent Captain Edward Hutchinson with twenty men to *Quawbaug* (Brookfield, Massachusetts) on July 28, 1675, *"to treat with several Sachems in those parts in order to the public peace."* They arrived in the village three days later, after a fifty mile hike, and found the *Nipmet* Indians peaceful. The Brookfield villagers seemed content and without fear of Indian attack. Next day, the 500 local Indians were to meet Hutchinson/for a *"powow,"* but instead they ambushed him and his men, killing eight and wounding five. The survivors ran to the village to warn the inhabitants, with the *Nipmets* close behind them. Some eighty settlers crowded into Ayer's Tavern, which remained their defensive fortress as savages flooded the village, burning and pillaging. *"That night,"* reports Captain Thomas Wheeler, *"they did war against us like so many wild bulls, sending in their shot amongst us till they attempted to fire the tavern, by hay and other combustible matter. Men went out and quenched the flames, but two were wounded. We feared we'd run out of ammunition and supplies, so we sent a messenger, Ephraim Curtis, but twice he was chased back. On the third attempt he snuck away and got to Marlborough, where he alerted all. During daylight they were less active, but at darkness they attacked again and fired the roof. . ."* The settlers then cut holes in the ceiling and roof of the tavern and put out the fires. Then the Indians lit hay around the tavern, and says Wheeler, *"we were forced to break down the wall of the tavern against the fire to put it out. . . Then they took a farm-cart, filled it with hay and set it on fire and pushed it against the tavern, but it rained and the fire went out. We were exhausted and suffocated by smoke, and that night, two of our women gave birth to twins."* On the third day of the seige, an army of 46 men under Captain James Parker of Groton arrived and the Indians retreated into the woods. Brookfield was completely in shambles, only the tavern and one half-built house remained standing.

At Marlborough, 25 miles from Brookfield, a combined force of

Nipmets and *Wampanoags* scalped a nine year old shepherd boy, Christopher Muchin, but he lived, and they cut off the hands of Phillip Curtice, *"and placed the hands upon a crotched pole at the wigwam door, faced against each other."*

Captain Mosley and his 110 men were ordered to march to Brookfield, *"and thence to seek the enemy in the woods near Lancaster."* At Lancaster, on August 22nd, *Nipmets* attacked and killed eight settlers, two of them children. Two days later, Springfield, Massachusetts was attacked by *Metacomet's* Indians, and thirty homes were destroyed, and many settlers were killed, but Mosley and his men arrived too late. They found only one old Indian woman in the surrounding woods, who told Mosley that *Metacomet* planned to destroy all frontier settlements first, then he would march to the coast and push the English into the sea. Mosley let his dogs loose on the old squaw and they chewed her to pieces.

"Our soldiers could never meet with any of the savages," wrote one of Mosley's men, *"but only drove them further westward, where they gathered all the Indians they could to their party about Pecomptuck"* (Deerfield). At Hatfield, they met up with a group of local Indians and there was a three hour fight, during which nine soldiers and 26 Indians were killed. On the same day, August 26th, Captain Beers with 36 soldiers was ambushed by *Nipmets* at *Squakeag* (Northfield), and all but eight soldiers were killed in the battle. They retreated to Hadley, Massachusetts, which was headquarters for the Connecticut troops.

Deerfield was attacked by *Metacomet's* men on September 14th. The settlers were forced to abandon their homes, plus 3,000 bushels of wheat that was being preserved in the fields. Four days later, Captain Tom Lathrop of Beverly, with a company of eighty men from Essex County, Massachusetts, was sent to Deerfield with 18 teamsters and their carts to gather the wheat and bring it to Hadley. It was a hot day, and their mission all but completed, when they stopped the carts filled with wheat at Muddy Brook, South Deerfield, to feast on wild grapes that were growing on vines near the road. Most of the soldiers unfortunately left their muskets in the carts as they walked deeper into the woods munching on the grapes. They were ambushed by some 700 Indians, coming at them from all directions. Captain Lathrop was one of the first to fall, then the teamsters and all the soldiers but seven were killed. John Toppan of Newbury, after being wounded, fell and covered himself with weeds, *"so that the Indians couldn't see me, and sometimes they stepped right over me."* He survived. Another was Henry Bodwell, who, with a musketball lodged in his left arm, battled the Indians by swinging a musket *"and made it through the line of Indians."* A third man who survived the massacre was Robert Dutch of Ipswich. He was shot in the head, half scalped and left for dead, miraculously he lived. Lathrop's company was called *"The Flower of Essex,"* for most of them were teenagers, and not one of them was over 22 years of age— Muddy Brook was renamed *"Bloody Brook."*

Mosley and his men were only a few miles away, near Deerfield, when they heard the gunfire coming from Muddy Brook. They marched on the double, and arrived in time to see *Metacomet's* savages cutting open bags of wheat, and stripping the bodies of the Essex men. Mosley attacked, but he was outnumbered seven to one. *Nipmet Sachem, One-Eyed Monoco,* who recognized Mosley, shouted, *"Come on Mosley, you want Indians? Here are Indians for you!"* Mosley was about to retreat, for many of his men were falling around him, but just as the sun was setting, Connecticut's Major Treat, with 100 soldiers and 60 *Mohigans* showed up. *Monoco* and his Indians retreated into the woods. Next day, *Monoco* and his warriors attacked the Deerfield garrison, where only 25 soldiers were on duty. One innovative soldier instead of firing his musket, blew a bugle, and *Monoco* again called a retreat. He had lost 96 of his warriors to Mosley the day before, and apparently thought the bugle was calling Mosley back again. Hatfield and Springfield were attacked again before the snow set in, but *"were bravely repulsed by settlers and soldiers."* *Metacomet,* who never led an Indian raid, but planned them all, then returned to the coast with his *Wampanoags* to spend the winter, and to convince the *Narragansetts* to join him in the war.

The *Narragansetts* had promised Major Savage in July that they would turn over any *Wampanoags* that entered their villages to the Boston or Plymouth authorities, and Governors Leverett and Winslow feared the worse, for no *Wampanoag* prisoners had arrived from *Canonicus.* Rumor from the *praying Indians* was that *Metacomet* with his tribe was living with the *Narragansetts* in their *Great Swamp* at South Kingston, Rhode Island. A Commission of *"United Colonies"* met at Boston and raised a troop of 1,000 men from all the New England territories, and placed them under the command of Governor Winslow. Just before Christmas, they marched to *Pocasset Neck* in Kingston. Storming through the frozen boggy woods for seven miles, they came to a great fortress of timbers, with many sharpened stakes pointing out at the invading colonists, and a deep water moat all around it. Inside this palisade, which seemed impregnable, were five acres of 600 wigwams, corn storage shacks, and 3,000 *Narragansetts* and *Wampanoags,* including *Canonicus* and *Metacomet*. The only entrance was a felled log, large enough for only one man to pass over it, lying across the broad moat. Three men tried to cross this log bridge single-file, and they were immediately shot dead by the Indians, firing at them from inside the fortress. Four more then tried and they too were punctured with arrows and musketballs.

Finally one soldier made it, then another and another. One managed to throw a firebrand inside, setting a wigwam on fire, and soon, the entire fortress was ablaze. One at a time, members of the Colonial army entered the great fortress, fighting Indians hand-to-hand to gain a footing so that more soldiers could enter. Inside, Indian squaws and their children were running and screaming, some with their winter furs ablaze. The Indians were *"dead in heaps upon ye snow,"* one soldier later reported. All the wigwams and storage bins went up in flames, and many cowering women and children were consumed with them. Captains Church and Mosley tried to save some of the stored corn so that their hungry men could eat it, but everything was burning.

Over 700 *Narragansetts* and *Wampanoags* died, and some 100 surrendered to Winslow, but *Canonicus* and *Metacomet*, with many of their warriors, managed to escape over the back fence of the fortress, and paddled away on barges that they constructed for just such an emergency. *Squaw Sachem Weetamo* of the *Pocassets*, however, drowned when her raft capsized. Her body washed ashore. The soldiers decapitated her, and placed her head on a pole at Taunton, where some of the *Pocasset* captives cried aloud when they spotted it, *"there is the head of our queen."* Most of the Indians who died in *"The Great Swamp Fight,"* were women and children, less than half were warriors. The United Colonial troops lost 80 men, with 152 wounded, but during their 18 mile trek from the swamp to Wickford, Rhode Island through a blinding snowstorm, eleven more froze to death and many were frostbitten.

Metacomet, with some 300 *Wampanoag* warriors, paddled their crude rafts to the Taunton River and disembarked near Dighton, then walked to *Nipmet* country. A few weeks later, *Canonicus* sent some 3,000 *Narragansett* warriors, under the charge of his nephew, *Canonchet*, to Mount Wachusett, north of Worcester, to join *Metacomet*. The *Wampanoag Sachem* was so pleased with this addition to his depleated army that he made *Canonchet* his military leader, over all the *Nipmets, Wampanoags*, and the few *Massachusetts* tribe members who had rallied to his cause. Except for Connecticut's *Mohigans* and the *praying Indians*, *Metacomet* was enticing warriors from all New England tribes, which greatly surprised and disturbed the Colonials. In many frontier settlements, all Indians were suspected of being allies to *Metacomet.* At about the same time of *"The Great Swamp Fight,"* Major Dennison of Andover reported to Governor Leverett that, *"it is hardly imaginable the panic-fear that is upon our upland plantations and scattered places."*

Governor Leverett and his War Commissioners decided to draft young men into the army, setting a quota to be met by every town and village. Many, especially those that lived in coastal towns, were opposed to the draft, and eligible sons were hidden in the woods or sent to sea to avoid it. Quakers not only refused to serve in the Colonial Army, but started an anti-war movement. Boston draft-dodgers were fined five-pounds, and Quakers were often beaten through the streets. Of the 5,000 men who were finally recruited, 500 were killed or captured by hostile Indians. Leverett also decided to supplement the draftees with a company of *praying Indians,* and 52 of them were recruited, one being *Job Nesutan,* who was 86 years old. For every enemy Indian they killed, they would receive a coat with brass buttons, and for killing *Metacomet,* the bounty was twenty coats.

Canonchet proved to be an able General for *Metacomet,* a master strategist in guerrilla warfare and highly skilled at hit-and-run techniques. After the heavy snows of January, 1676, he led some 300 chosen warriors to hit Lancaster, Massachusetts again. Mary Rowlandson, wife of the local minister, was one of the first to see them coming from a window in the garrison-house. *"It was Sunrise,"* she later wrote, *"and the murderous wretches came, burning and destroying all before them. The bullets seemed to fly like hail. The Indians set fire to the house, and some in our house fought for their lives, others wallowed in their blood. . . I took my children and one of my sister's, to go forth and leave the house, the fire increasing, and coming along behind us, roaring, and the Indians gaping before us with their guns, spears, and hatchets to devour us. No sooner were we out of the house, but my brother-in-law fell down dead, and the Indians were presently upon us. The bullets flying thick, one went through my side, and the same through the bowels and hand of my dear child in my arms. . ."* Lancaster was burned to the ground, 26 settlers were killed, and 24, including Mary Rowlandson, were taken captive, *"dragged along day and night by the savages."* Six of her eight children were killed by the Indians, *"some shot, some stabbed with spears, and some knocked down with their hatchets."* She and her surviving two children were later ransomed.

Immediately after the Lancaster massacre, *Canonchet* attacked Medfield, burning all the houses there, and killing 20 settlers. Next was Marlborough, where the settlers had rebuilt their homes after being invaded the year before. *Canonchet* waited until Sunday morning, when the villagers were at church service to attack again. His warriors burned 13 houses, 11 barns, and killed all the cattle, but slew and scalped only one man, before retreating to the next town, Sudbury. Marlborough men raised the alarm by riding to neighboring villages, and one rode to Boston, where the Governor immediately dispatched forty men under Captain Samuel Wadsworth of Milton, to stop *Canonchet's* rampage. Twelve men from Concord, who got to Sudbury before Wadsworth, were ambushed and slaughtered. After marching some 25 miles, Wadsworth allowed his men to rest momentarily near Green Hill at Sudbury, but they soon realized they were surrounded and vastly outnumbered by *Narragansetts* and *Nipmets*. The Colonials retreated to the top of Green Hill, but the Indians closed in, killing 29 men, including Captain Wadsworth, and capturing six, who were cruelly tortured that night of April 19, 1676. They cut a hole in the stomach of one soldier, pulled out his intestines, and tied them to a horse's tail, then burned the horse so it would gallop off in panic and pain, the soldier dragging behind it. Only 14 of Wadsworth's men, which included part of the Marlborough militia, managed to sneak off Green Hill that night and hide in a nearby mill, saved next morning by a company of soldiers from Watertown.

Metacomet's men attacked Groton on March 13, burning 65 houses, but only one resident was killed. *Sachem One-Eyed Monoco* shouted to those locked up in the well fortified garrison-house at Groton, before he retreated. *"I will now burn down Cambridge and Boston,"* he warned, and *Monoco* came close to keeping his word. The combined force of *Wampanoags, Narragansetts,* and *Nipmets,* hit Weymouth, Dorchester, and Clark's garrison-house, only three miles from Plymouth, where they killed eleven men. Then they proceeded to burn and pillage Rhode Island from the seacoast to Providence. At Providence, 77-year-old Roger Williams went out alone to meet the attacking Indians, asking them not to destroy the homes. *"Williams, you are a good man,"* said Canonchet, *"not a hair of your head will be touched,"* but he promised no more.

On June 2nd, Connecticut's Major John Talbot, with soldiers and *Mohigans,* met up with some 300 *Narragansetts* on the Rhode Island coast, and slaughtered 240 of them. The others were taken captive, and the *Mohigans,* with permission from Talbot, were allowed to torture some of them. Talbot describes the torture of one *Narragansett,* *"who boasted that he had killed 19 Englishmen. . . The Mohigans first circled him, then cut off one of his fingers; then they cut another and another, until they had dismembered one hand, the blood sometimes spurting out in streams a yard from his hand . . . They then dealt with his toes, all the while making himself dance around the circle and sing. At last they broke the bones of his legs, for which he was forced to sit down, till they had knocked out his brains."*

About the same time, *Canonchet* and some 300 *Narragansetts* and *Nipmets* were being chased down at Pawtucket, Rhode Island. Being pursued, *Canonchet* fell into a stream, soaking himself and ruining his trusty musket. Not able to fire back at the young soldier, Robert Staunton, who aimed his musket at the great warrior, *Canonchet* threw up his hands and said to Staunton, *"You are like a child, you no understand war."* *Canonchet* was offered his life if he'd ask all his Narragansetts to surrender. He answered *"No! I shall die before my heart is soft."* The *praying Indians* and *Mohigans* shot him and then cut his body into four parts and burned it, saving only his head, which was presented to the people of Hartford.

Captain Ben Church received word from a *praying Indian* that *Metacomet* had retreated back to his village at Mount Hope. With a small detachment of soldiers and *praying Indians,* Church went there. On August 12, the *Wampanoag Sachem* was spotted in the woods accompanied by only two of his tribe. Church had them surrounded. When *Metacomet* spied the *praying Indians* waiting in ambush, he charged at them. A *praying Indian* named *Alderman,* took aim and shot the *King of the Wampanoags* in the chest, providing him an instant death. Those with *Metacomet* were killed as well.

Indian *Alderman* then chopped off *Metacomet's* right hand, which he kept as a prize for his entire life, displaying it for hand-outs from village to village, and preserving it in a bucket of rum. *Metacomet's* left hand was cut off to present to Governor Leverett, and his feet were delivered to Providence, Rhode Island. His body was halved, then quartered and hung in a nearby tree. His head was cut off and brought to Plymouth, where it was carried around on a pole in a great celebration. The head remained in Plymouth, displayed on the pole in the middle of town for 25 years, the skull eventually becoming a nesting place for birds. One day, the most reverent Increase Mather, President of Harvard College, climbed the pole and removed *Metacomet's* jaw-bone, throwing it to the ground, shouting, *"this King Philip was a blasphemous liviathon."*

With the death of Metacomet, *"The Great Indian War"* was over, his few remaining warriors scattering into the woods, some retreating to the wilds of Maine and Canada. Governor Leverett announced that all Indians who did not kill anyone during the war, would be granted amnesty. The few *Metacomet* warriors that did surrender, were sold into salvery. Two of *Metacomet's Panieses, Tuspaquin,* who was married to *Metacomet's* sister, and *Anawam,* surrendered when they were promised that they would not be harmed. *Tuspaquin,* known as *"The Black Sachem,"* had bragged during the war that he was bullet-proof, so Winslow had him shot at Plymouth, as proof to other Indians that he was not. *Anawam* was beheaded. *Metacomet's* wife and nine year old son were captured and shipped off to the West Indies as slaves, although Mather wanted them executed. Thousands of Indians of the *Massachusetts, Pennacook,* and *Nashuba* tribes, many of whom were in prisoner-of-war camps during the war, even though they had sworn neutrality, were also shipped off as slaves to the West Indies.

There was still insecurity and fear among the settlers, and it was an unsteady peace, with frontier villages being attacked now and then by renegade warriors, and then, twelve years after *Metacomet's* uprising, came the French and Indian War. On September 23, 1676, there was an alarm that thousands of Indians were about to attack Boston. Some 1,200 men were armed and waiting by twelve noon, but a half hour later a messenger arrived in Boston, telling the Governor that it had been a false alarm. A sentry at Mendon, thirty miles away, had *"mistakenly fired the alarm, while drunk."*

The last white man to talk to *Metacomet* had been missionary John Eaton. His last words to Eaton were *"We the Indians had been the first in doing good to the English, and the English were first in doing us wrong. My neck can not bear the yoke. I must walk free beneath the sun."* King Philip however, did not heed the last words of the great *Powahee Passaconnaway,* and he caused *"the mischief"* the *Powahee* had warned about. Thus, he *"was rooted off the earth."* Today, some 300 years later, you and I walk *free beneath the sun,* on what was once the Indians' cherished homeland.

(Bibliography available by writing the Publisher.)